A Mom's Guide to
Life After Divorce

To James

All the best!

Becky

A Mom's Guide to
Life After Divorce

Move Forward to the Life You Want

Becky Adams

FLOURISH
PRESS

San Diego, California

Published by Flourish Press, Inc.
3525 Del Mar Heights Road, #383
San Diego, CA 92130 USA
Telephone: 800-450-5390
www.FlourishPress.com
For special orders or bulk purchases, please contact Flourish Press.

Publisher's Cataloging-in-Publication data

Adams, Rebecca Lynn.
    A Mom's guide to life after divorce: move forward to the life you want / Becky Adams.
    p. cm.
    ISBN 978-0-9849920-1-0
1. Divorce. 2. Divorced parents. 3. Divorced women. 4. Children of divorced parents.
I. Title.

HQ834 .A33 2015
306.89/082 --dc23   2015935179

Editing by Author Bridge Media
Book Cover Design by Peri Poloni-Gabriel, Knockout Design
Book Interior Design and Layout by Donna D'Angelo
First Edition
Printed in the United States of America

For *you.*

. . . .

Because this book is dedicated to you, there's something I want you to know:

Thank you for doing all the things you do that nobody else knows about or notices; the things it takes to keep your kids' lives running smoothly. Thank you for making sure they are fed, clothed, sheltered, nurtured, appreciated, and most of all, loved. Thank you for keeping them organized so they go to school with the supplies they need, for all the permission slips you fill out, and for the extra cash you slip them—yes, *all* of that.

Nobody else will thank you. Eventually, one day, your kids will understand the effort it took to make all of those things happen. But right now, you're probably operating alone, without anyone else recognizing or appreciating all you do.

I know what you are doing. I know how difficult it can be. So from me to you…thank you.

. . . .

Contents

· · · · · · · · · ·

PART THREE: Get Going — Live It Every Day

Foreword

You never planned to have children with someone and then divorce him. Who does? What could be more contradictory to what you'd hoped for your children? In all the years you spent anticipating your children's needs, feathering a safe nest for them to grow up in, and encouraging them to be their most authentic and happiest self, you *never* imagined them involved a divorce. It wasn't part of the plan. It never is.

As a mother, your child's welfare has always been your top priority. Yet when you go through a divorce, your resources and sense of identity are strained. At the time your child needs you most, you may feel tapped out and completely baffled as to what to do.

So many mothers have walked in your shoes. That's why, as a marriage and family therapist, I am so grateful for Becky Adams' book, *A Mom's Guide to Life After Divorce*. It's easy to use, and it's a much-needed resource for how to stabilize your life and your child's life, and move forward after your divorce.

In your hands is a compassionate self-help tool for both you and your child. So much pain, frustration, and many false starts can be avoided if you use this book as a guide to create a new, productive life for you and your child.

Save your energy. You don't have to reinvent the wheel. Just follow the simple steps in this book — kindly written by someone who has already experienced your journey — and tailor each step to you and your child's needs.

A Mom's Guide to Life After Divorce has already laid the groundwork for how to structure your post-divorce life in an efficient way to conserve your energy and time. Like plans for a building, it's helpful to have a basic starter plan so you're free to tailor the future you and your child will share together.

By using this book as a starter plan, you will minimize unnecessary pain for you and your child. Your child's happiness depends very much on the proactive choices you make now, during this crucial transition, as you create an entirely new family structure.

Parenting your kids after your divorce is a challenge under the best of circumstances. As one household is split into two, choices concerning your child are less automatic. Suddenly, decisions like where and when your child should be dropped off after soccer practice and who will take your child to school on what day must be reevaluated.

The result of your child living in two households is that there are now twice as many chances for things to go wrong — and yet you have double the number of opportunities to get things right when it comes to the domestic minutiae that affect your child.

Direct communication between you and your former spouse regarding the coordination of your child's social calendar, medical needs, education, and where clean clothes will be kept for the next school day is now open to re-negotiation. Much of the fabric of how things got done before will be re-woven into a new pattern out of necessity.

How can you tip the scale to favor your child's well-being? There are so many ways. You have to do this one way or another, so why not do it well? Think of *A Mom's Guide to Life After Divorce* as a heartfelt accelerator to your healing.

MICHELLE PIPER, MS, LMFT

Introduction

You're probably feeling a little freaked out right now. The decision to divorce does that to us.

You might also feel afraid of what's to come, overwhelmed by all the changes that need to take place in your life, and worried about your kids' well-being. You could be angry and resentful that this is even happening. Or scared to death that you won't be able to pick yourself up and move on with your life.

And that's just the emotional stuff.

There are also the practical worries. Will you be moving to a new place? Will your child custody schedule be workable? Can you manage your finances? Can you juggle all the demands of being a single parent?

And then there are the daily frustrations of parenting kids that live in two homes. Where is your daughter's soccer uniform? The materials for the science project were left at the other house. You're leaving for vacation, and the kids' passports are at Dad's place. The permission slip for the senior class trip requires both parents' signatures, and it is due tomorrow. It goes on and on.

The challenges mount and the frustration feels endless.

I've been there. I've stumbled down the dark street of the divorce process, and the weeks, months, and years that follow. But in the end, all that stumbling led me somewhere. I learned how to restructure my life in a way that works well. I figured out ways to move forward from emotional pain, handle practical worries, and work my way through daily frustrations.

I learned how to get down that street by taking it one step at a time. Some steps felt solid; some felt shaky. But I kept going. You can, too.

You can do this

Light is waiting for you at the end of the long, dark street you're on. And this book will help you find it.

I paid attention to what worked and didn't work as I went through this process myself, and I documented it, so your walk down this street can be easier. So you'll have the information you need to move ahead confidently with your life and come out on the other side better than you can even imagine at the moment.

Chances are, you could use a little encouragement right about now, a little support, the message that you will be all right. You may not believe it right now, but you will. You've got this. If I can do this, you can, too.

And if you don't believe in yourself right now, just start by believing me.

My story

I grew up on a farm in a family of hard workers. That's where I got my deep-rooted belief that I can figure things out using common sense and persistence. I got married in college. We didn't have any kids, so when the marriage dissolved when I was in my early thirties, it made the *ending* part a lot easier than if we had.

I struggled after that, though. I felt shaken and fragile. I lived far away from my family, so I had to figure out how to heal and recover on my own. I started therapy and began to develop little strategies for how to get my life moving again.

I married again a few years later and had my daughter a few years after that. I was in my mid-forties when my second marriage ended. This time there was a child involved, and that made things very different. This time, I had to be solid and stable.

My former spouse and I agreed to share custody of our daughter, so that meant there would be a lot of changes to both my life and hers. I needed to figure out a way for all of this to work so she was impacted as little as possible, and so I could do the best job of being a single parent.

Because I had a lot of questions, I consulted a divorce lawyer to educate myself on what to expect. I wanted to know everything I could so that I would understand what was going to happen. We hit it off during the meeting, and in a strange turn of events, even though I wasn't looking for a new job, she offered me one. So I joined her firm, not having any prior experience in family law.

What I got from my experience working at her law firm ended up being an incredible gift. The heartache, pain, resentment, and revenge I saw in people getting divorced gave me a clear picture of what I *didn't* want in my life. And that was the beginning of a belief that I could do this differently. I just needed to be strategic and organized about it.

It didn't come easily, though. I remember sitting in my car at the beach one day at lunch time, feeling overwhelmed by everything that was changing in my life. It felt like the breeze blowing through the car window could knock me over. Words, when they came out of my mouth, felt like they were coming from someplace else. And I was most scared of how the divorce would impact my daughter. I walked around in that state of mind for weeks.

And then one day, as I was pulling into the grocery store parking lot, I wondered, "How would my friends describe me?" And it came to me: like an anchor. I was the steady, predictable person people came to when they were hurting or needed help. I was an anchor for my daughter. I was an anchor for a lot of people at work. Why couldn't I be an anchor for myself?

It was so simple, and yet so powerful. *Yes,* I thought. *I can do that.* And at that moment, I *knew* I was going to be okay.

The simple decision that I was going to be okay was a game-changer for me. I remember clearly how different things felt the next day. My coffee tasted better. The sky looked brighter. It was as if somebody had turned on the lights in what had felt like a very dark place.

After that, I began to stabilize and organize my life. I'm an organized person by nature. I create systems for how to do things — figuring out the most effective and efficient way to get things done. Using the information I learned at the law firm, combined with my innate ability for organization, I assembled a system of practical ways to make things easier in my new life as a single parent.

Then, a few years later, an idea started brewing in me. That idea was this book. I wanted to share what I learned during those years at the family law firm, and in the weeks, months, and years that followed while raising my daughter — a kid that lived in two homes. I wanted to help you get through not just the tough spots, but *all* the spots. So you can make it to the end of the road knowing that somebody else has gone first and done it before, and will light the way for you.

How to read this book

The information written here is an expression of how I look at life. There are ideas that have been tried and practiced by me, and there are lessons I've observed and learned from others.

This book has three parts, each one offering different ways to move on from your divorce while minimizing the impact that this big life change has on your kids. The first part, *Get Stabilized,* will help you heal from your current situation and become solid and stable. The second part, *Get Organized,* gives practical ideas for how to get organized so your new reality works for you and things become easier. And the third part, *Get Going—Live It Every Day,* gives strategies to keep growing in a way that will allow you to live your life fully. Each part is broken down into chapters that give specific suggestions and examples of how to hit each of these goals.

This book is probably best if read from start to finish because that logically follows my path through the information, but it can also be read randomly, one chapter at a time. Read it however works best for you. Some chapters may resonate with you right now, and some may not. You may be ready to implement some of these ideas, and others you may need to come back for later.

I suggest you let the book meet you wherever you are. And wherever that is, is perfect.

My promise to you

It takes a lot of personal growth to get to the point where you're healing, better organized, and ready to move ahead with your life. This book is a path for growth, and the chapters are like the streetlights on that dark street you're traveling, helping you get from here to there.

I promise you that the information here will make a difference. The simple act of stabilizing and organizing your life will allow you to grow into someone far beyond what you may think is possible right now. If you follow these steps, you will come out on the other end of your divorce a stronger, healed, organized person who is getting on with her life.

Stick around, and I'll show you how.

1

Get Stabilized

CHAPTER 1

Make the Initial Adjustment

You're braver than you believe, and stronger than you seem, and smarter than you think.
— A.A. MILNE

* * * * * * *

I remember staring at the back of the door after it closed. It was the first time my former husband came to take our daughter to be with him for the weekend. The sense of finality hit me like a ton of bricks. This was going to be my life. This was how it was going to be. The emptiness of the space around me pressed down like a tangible weight. The air felt so heavy, I thought I might choke. I memorized the shape of the wood molding on the door. Two small rectangles on the top and two big rectangles on the bottom. It was painted white and had a silver doorknob.

I hoped that maybe if I didn't move, the whole thing might be a dream. It might not really be happening. But slowly reality came, and I knew I had to take a few steps and start to move.

I made myself a cup of tea and sat down at my kitchen table. Everything was in order. The dishes were done, the kitchen was clean. Why hadn't I waited and finished them after my daughter was gone, so I had something to do to kill the long stretch of time that was between me and when she came back again in 47.9 hours? I heard the ticking of the clock on the wall and the sound of kids playing down the street. I sat and sat and sat and just looked around, frozen. And finally, the tears came, rolling down my cheeks. First just a few, and then a steady stream. *Let them come,* I thought.

This was a big day in my life—the start of a major transition for me, and the beginning of something new and completely different. I needed to figure out a way to adapt to my new life and begin to stabilize myself for what was ahead.

But at that moment, I had no idea how to do that.

I'd been through tough times before. I'd experienced heartache at other times in my life that left me feeling shaky and disconnected from the solid, centered feeling I typically had. But I knew this time, I had to access every resource I'd discovered, and every positive behavior tool I had in my personal bag of tricks to pull myself forward from this sense of immobility. I had a daughter to consider this time, and I needed to be in the best shape possible to provide a stable, secure home for both of us.

So I decided to do what I've always done: I started with the basics of what I've learned over a lifetime. Focus on the next thing in front of me. Put a plan together for what I wanted my day to be like. Figure out what would feel good and useful to accomplish. And take loving care of myself. To accomplish all of this, I used all of the things I will describe in this section, and I started to create a sense of stability. Stabilizing myself felt like the key to moving forward. Without that, I would be in no shape to pull off the job of being a single parent.

❂ ❂ ❂ ❂ ❂ ❂ ❂ ❂

In this first section of the book, *Get Stabilized,* I describe a lot of different things that helped me move forward and stabilize my life when I was going through my divorce. There are ideas here that will give you a new perspective on everything from your daily routine, to taking care of yourself and healing, to working with your former spouse to raise your children together.

So here you are—separated or divorced, or maybe soon to be one of those. Maybe it has been coming for a long time, or maybe it happened unexpectedly. Either way, when it happens, life feels surreal—kind of like, "What the heck just happened?" One day you are going along in your life, and the next day everything is different. I know it felt that way for me.

So where are you? What happened? It doesn't matter if you are the one who initiated the divorce or not; the reality is, things are different now. And the world will feel different, at least for a while, until you can stabilize yourself and reorganize the structure of your life.

Divorce is a time of enormous change. It is the ultimate transition—moving from married to single, from one lifestyle to another, from one family structure to a new one. So many things are different.

And with all those differences comes the need to adjust and to stabilize yourself and your kids' lives so you can move forward to a new and happy life. Taking time to get really stabilized, by clearly understanding what's changing in your life, taking steps to heal emotionally from what's happening and helping your kids to get stabilized is the first crucial step in moving forward.

Without stabilization, it's easy to get stuck, or immobilized like I was feeling in my life. When that happens, we aren't able to effectively care for ourselves or our kids, or to create that new and happy life we all want to have.

When one family and one household is divided in two, it won't feel the same. The housing, childcare, schedules, finances, and communication needs are different. Essentially, everything is different. And that may feel unsettling at first.

If you are sharing custody of your kids with your former spouse, you will be alone at times now. If you haven't been the primary caregiver for your children, you may now need to take a more active role as a parent. You may now live in a different house, possibly smaller than the one you lived in before. Your financial situation might change a lot. And the household stuff you had before is probably being divided up.

It is normal to feel off-balance right now. You may feel angry or afraid or maybe even completely numb. And just like the stages of grief that we go through when somebody we love dies, there are stages of grief related to our divorce. You may be feeling some or all of these stages, or you might be jumping back and forth between them as you adjust to your new life.

Denial is when we struggle to believe our divorce is even happening in the first place. Sometimes we deny that we are in any emotional pain and continue to say, "I'm just fine."

Anger can happen if we feel our "happily ever after" is over, our life is changing, our financial circumstances are different, or that we have to do things we don't want to. And sometimes we are angry with ourselves for putting up with bad behavior for too long or not seeing the signs that our marriage was over.

Bargaining happens when we ask ourselves things like, "What if?" or tell ourselves, "If only..." We may ask, "What if I had been more concerned about how he felt?" or "If only I had acted on the problem before it got too big to resolve." At this stage, we often try to make a deal with ourselves about—or try to repair—things that have already happened.

Depression is when we feel a deep sadness about the loss of our marriage, and also when the physical and emotional symptoms of our divorce come crashing in. In this stage, we sometimes have trouble doing regular daily activities, like eating and sleeping, and we are often overwhelmed with worry about what will happen to us. This stage can feel scary and leave us feeling uncertain about what to do next.

Acceptance takes place when we realize our marriage is over, and it's time for us to move on. It doesn't mean that we won't feel sad or angry anymore; it means we've accepted—or have started to accept—that our divorce will happen. At this point, we can begin to move forward.

Sometimes, while trying *not* to feel the pain of our situation, we rush to the next stage. And just like other things in life, accepting and adjusting to something new takes time.

In order to move ahead and heal emotionally, we have to let go of what was, and trust that wherever we are in this process is exactly where we are supposed to be. We can't get to the next stage by skipping some of the steps or taking a detour. Each step is there for a reason. And each step will lead to the next. Be patient. This transition is leading to an important place — your new beginning.

Be gentle with yourself as you become aware of the stages you may be going through, and some of the things you may be feeling. You will feel strange and unsettled for a while. But you are going to be okay. There are things you can do to get stabilized as you wind your way through this time of your life. The rest of the chapters in this book will be your streetlights along what may seem, right now, like a long, dark road. I've been down this road, and I know how to help light the way.

All of these strategies are designed to help you regain a sense of strength about your life that, in turn, will create a sense of stability for your kids. I'll take you through these strategies one by one, and tell you why each of them is important. If you follow along and implement them in your life, I promise that you will gain a sense of confidence and empowerment that you probably don't have right now.

ACTION ITEM

As you go through your day today, be aware of how you are feeling. Notice your emotional state of mind — the high points and the lows. Remind yourself during the low points that a lot is changing in your life, and that this may contribute to feeling unsettled. Be grateful for the times when you are in the high places. You'll undoubtedly feel both as you adjust to and accept that your divorce is happening.

CHAPTER 2

Know the Details of Your Situation

When we know better, we do better.
—MAYA ANGELOU

. . . .

Cheryl stepped out of her meeting to call her next-door neighbor, Beth. She'd just received an urgent text saying "Call me right away." She dialed quickly and asked what was so important. "Don't freak out," Beth said, "but there's a bright orange foreclosure notice posted on the front door of your house."

Cheryl felt as if she'd been punched in the gut. Foreclosure? That could only mean one thing—the mortgage on her house hadn't been paid. Cheryl and her husband Tim were divorcing, and paying the mortgage was supposed to be his responsibility. Apparently he hadn't been doing that.

Cheryl frantically dialed Tim's number. He didn't answer, so she left a message on his phone. What was going on? Her mind was racing.

She logged into their joint bank account. With all of the changes happening in her life, she hadn't checked the balance on that account in months. Her heart sank. Zero balance. So she checked the mortgage account. No access. Panic was setting in now.

Then she called the mortgage company and discovered she no longer had access to their mortgage information. A sick feeling began to settle in the pit of Cheryl's stomach. And slowly, things started to become clear. Things that had seemed out of the ordinary for the last few months started to make sense.

Tim had been buying lots of new furniture and things for his new apartment; things that seemed too expensive for Tim's salary. At the time, Cheryl had a feeling she should check out those "out of the ordinary" things, but she had disregarded her instincts because they'd always managed their finances separately.

They shared just one account—managed by Tim—for the household expenses they'd agreed to share. Instead of paying their mortgage though, Tim had been buying furniture and things for his apartment. Plus, he'd changed the access to their mortgage account, so Cheryl hadn't been getting the delinquent notices.

Cheryl discovered their mortgage was over six months past due. She was eventually able to borrow money from her parents, bring the mortgage account current, and stop the foreclosure.

Months later, thinking back on the situation, Cheryl realized that she should have listened to her instincts all along instead of disregarding how she felt. But she had been so distracted by their divorce that she hadn't taken the time to check that things were happening as they should. It was a painful lesson for Cheryl to learn.

* * * * * * * *

I don't want you to experience a terrible surprise like Cheryl. Make yourself aware of all the details related to your divorce and how your life will change, and you will gain a sense of personal empowerment. You'll know what to expect. Nothing will blindside you, and you'll know where you stand. And that sense of personal stability will help your kids remain stable during the transition as well.

There are quite a few crucial questions you will need to have answers for. This list might seem a bit overwhelming at first. If it does, just focus on finding the answers to one section at a time.

Your Divorce Agreement
- Do you understand all the details of your agreement?
- If it hasn't been finalized already, do you know the date when your divorce will be final?

Child Custody
- Are you clear about your child custody agreement and arrangements (physical, legal, etc.)?
- What is the new custody schedule?
- Have you created a parenting agreement for how you will work together to raise your kids?

Home and Living Arrangements
- Have your living arrangements changed? Do you need to move?
- If you have moved, will your kids need to change schools?
- Have you divided your household goods and furniture?
- Are there changes you should make for your physical safety? Change the door locks? Install an alarm?

Finances
- How has your financial situation changed?
- Do you know who is responsible for paying for what?

- Do you need to create a revised budget and plan for living within a new financial structure?
- Are there any equalizing payments that need to take place between you and your former spouse? What is the timing for these?
- Are there financial accounts that need to be closed or transferred into or out of your name?
- What are the tax implications of your divorce? Who takes the deduction for the children?
- What changes need to be made to your financial and online world? Have you changed your passwords?

Other Considerations

- Have you started working or changed jobs?
- Are there any loose ends that require action on your part?

Please keep in mind that this is just a partial list of questions. For a complete printable checklist with space to write your own answers, visit BeckyAdams.net/know-the-details.

These may seem like obvious questions, but a surprising number of people go through the divorce process and still aren't sure of the answers.

I thought about many of the things on the list when I was going through my divorce, but some of them never occurred to me. I've seen what can happen when people aren't paying attention, and I urge you to be 100 percent sure you know what's going on. When you take the time to educate yourself and clearly understand your situation, you free yourself from worrying about what might happen. In doing so, you also give yourself the opportunity to take the next step on the road to stabilization: giving yourself time and space to heal.

ACTION ITEM

Block out an afternoon and read through your divorce paperwork. Make sure you understand every single detail of the agreement with your former spouse, and that you're clear on the changes you will make in your life. If you aren't, make notes and check with your lawyer or mediator. Think of it as a gift you can give yourself—the gift of clarity. You are educating yourself, so you have the information you need to move forward in your life.

Now that you know this information, you're in a position to deal with it in a positive and productive way.

CHAPTER 3

Give Yourself Time to Heal

*Wherever you are right now is where you are
in your process of healing. And wherever you
are—you are showing up right on time.*
— LEEZA GIBBONS

. . . .

On the days she didn't have custody of her son, Vicki just couldn't go home right after work. It was too lonely and empty for her. It made her sad to go home to an empty house, or to go home alone, without her son—until she figured out a way to make the transition home at the end of the day easier for herself.

Vicki loved going to the movies. So when she was finished working on the days she was alone, she headed to the movie theater. There, she could relax and lose herself in the movie she had come to watch. There was something about allowing herself that stop-over time at the movie theater that just worked for her. Afterward, she was able to go home for the evening without the anxiety she felt if she tried to do it right after work.

Vicki went to hundreds of movies in the year or so following her divorce. Eventually, she adjusted to her new life and didn't need to go to the movies all the time. But it was a way for her to allow herself time to heal and to make a gentle shift to her new life.

. . . .

The process of grieving and healing from a divorce is like a crazy roller coaster ride. It doesn't stick to any particular timeline. Some days we feel like we are recovering, and the next day we feel worse than we did in the beginning. Then, some time later, we feel better again.

Giving ourselves time and space to heal from our divorce is an important thing to do. As I described in the "Make the Initial Adjustment" chapter, this time of your life involves a lot of transition and change. Adjusting to those changes will take time. When we allow time in our lives for healing, we are taking loving, responsible care of ourselves — something that maybe hasn't happened in a long time. That kind of care will allow healing to happen, and is an important step in stabilizing your life.

My experience has been that if you skip over this step — if you just keep saying to yourself, "I'm just fine" — the transition takes longer, and the pain and unhealed feelings seep out through the cracks later on.

It's important to take time to heal, and also to keep moving forward so we feel like we're making progress.

Give yourself time. During my divorce, there were two ways that worked well for me to allow healing time in my life. The first was to spend time alone, just *being*. Sometimes this meant sitting at a coffee shop, where I liked being in the company of other people, and where I could just think. Other times it was something like taking a long bath at night. Both allowed me the time to roll everything around in my mind, make sense of it all, and develop strategies for how to move forward with my life.

The second way was talking to friends and family on the phone at night after my daughter was in bed. Because I was working full-time, I found I could get through the day okay, but often I would hit a rough patch in the evenings when the house was quiet, and I was alone. I'm so grateful for the support of my sisters and friends during that time. A quick chat on the phone to get an injection of love and a nudge toward healing made a huge difference. I did it almost every night for months. As time went on, and I felt more emotionally healed, I didn't need to talk every night anymore.

What can we do with the time to heal? Here are a few things that worked well for me:

- **Ask yourself what you need.** Understanding what you need to do to take care of yourself is a very personal, individual thing. In her book, *The Language of Letting Go,* Melody Beattie suggests that we ask ourselves, especially in times of transition and change, "What do I need to do to take care of myself today or for this moment? What would demonstrate love and self-responsibility?" To determine what you need, ask yourself the following questions:

    - *Do I feel overwhelmed, stressed out? Have I been working too hard?* Maybe I need to take a day off, relax, and do something I enjoy.

    - *Have I been neglecting my job or daily tasks?* Then maybe what I need to do is get back into a routine.

* *Do I feel physically sick or run down?* Then I need to take time to buy healthy food and get a good night's sleep.

Nobody can tell us how to take care of ourselves. We must each listen to our internal guide. We need to ask, "What do I need to do to take loving, responsible care of myself?" Then we need to act on the answer.

- **Focus on what you *can* change.** You can't change the past or what happened to you. You can't change the decisions you made or how you behaved in a particular situation. You *can* change how you act in the future and focus on making decisions that serve you, your kids and your new life. Wouldn't you rather concentrate on the things you *can* change than on the things you can't?

- **Know that it's okay to have good days.** Sometimes we get stuck in our misery and, out of habit, stay in that place. But remember, during the process of healing, it is possible (and okay!) to have good days too. Celebrate and embrace these when they come along.

- **Ask what is the next right move?** Sometimes it's tough to figure out what to do next. The list of things you have to understand and adapt to may seem endless. So just keep it as simple as possible. Focus on the next thing in front of you: the next decision, the next phone call, the next errand to run. Keep moving, doing one thing at a time. Then you'll feel like you're making progress.

- **Get professional help.** Even if we do all the things suggested in this chapter—take loving care of ourselves, focus on what we can change, and keep moving forward—sometimes we still need help. Getting professional help, through a skilled therapist, counselor, or clergy member will make an enormous difference. A professional will give perspective, helpful advice, and coping ideas for your unique situation. This allows you to move forward and transition into your new life.

Part of healing is getting to the point where we understand how to help ourselves so we can feel stabilized. An important aspect of helping ourselves is realizing we are in control of our own lives. In the next chapter, I describe a way of thinking that will leave you feeling empowered about your life.

ACTION ITEM:

What is your personal recipe for self-care? What are the "go-to" things you rely on to lift your spirits?

If you don't have a list of these things, take some time to create one. Then, on the days when you feel blue or overwhelmed, you'll have a tried and true list of ways to help yourself feel better. Plan to give yourself one self-care item per week. Or more! Do as many as you need to take loving care of yourself.

CHAPTER 4

Realize You Are in Control of Your Life

The one thing you can't take away from me is the
way I choose to respond to what happens to me.
— VIKTOR E. FRANKL, *Man's Search for Meaning*

* * * * * * * *

I remember a time in my life when I felt I was a victim of my personal circumstances. Everything was changing in my world. I was getting divorced, changing my home, my job, and, as a result, a lot of my friends. My entire sense of community and support was uprooted and set back down in a different place.

I felt like my world was crumbling. And I was feeling very sorry for myself. But I also very clearly remember the day I decided that I would not fall victim to that kind of thinking. Instead, I decided: I am okay. I'm sitting right here in my house, and I'm okay. I'm completely on my own, and I'm okay. Everything in my world feels different, and I'm okay. Unlike so many other people in the world, I lead an extremely fortunate life. I am okay.

* * * * * * * *

Victor Frankl, a WWII concentration camp survivor, wrote about his experiences as an inmate at Auschwitz. In his book, *Man's Search for Meaning*, Frankl described what he learned while at Auschwitz: that our resilience and chances of survival depend on whether or not we have something to live and hope for in the future. He also suggested that our reactions aren't just a response to what's happening in our lives, but are also rooted in the freedom we have to choose our reaction—even in the midst of severe suffering.

I see a direct parallel between Frankl's theory and how we see ourselves during and after our divorce. If we see ourselves as a victim of our divorce, we tend to stay stuck and unable to move on with our lives. But if we see that we have a choice in how we respond to our situation, we have so much more personal power. When we choose to be responsible for ourselves and our lives—even if we've been wronged or the circumstances are unfair—we keep control of our lives in our own hands, and that creates a sense of stability for us.

Here's why:

We have choices every day about how to handle things— how to react to a particular situation, what words we use or what actions we take. When we choose a path that moves us in a direction that feels productive for us and our kids, one that moves us away from old feelings and behaviors that don't serve us well, we are choosing our new future. We are releasing ourselves from our past. And that allows us to move forward.

Unfortunate and challenging things happen to everybody, and most times they are things we would never choose. It's how we respond to what happens that makes the difference between being a victim and being a survivor, and that response is completely within our control.

Life happened to me. Life happened to you. Life happens to all of us. We can't control what we've been given, but we can control what we do with what we've been given. Always.

Taking good care of ourselves by nurturing our physical and emotional health is another step toward building stability for ourselves. When we do, we'll be in good shape to handle the adjustments that are coming our way. In the next chapter, I will show you how to do that.

> **ACTION ITEM**
>
> Tremendous power comes as a result of the realization that we are in control of our own lives and situations.
>
> Is there one area of your life right now where you are not reacting the way you want to? How could you change this today? Is there an area where you see yourself as a victim of the situation rather than as somebody who has a choice about how to react? What one action could you take to move from being a victim to creating a choice or option for yourself?

CHAPTER 5

Nurture Your Physical and Emotional Health

Gratitude unlocks the fullness of life. It turns what we have into enough, and more. It turns denial into acceptance, chaos to order, confusion to clarity. It can turn a meal into a feast, a house into a home, a stranger into a friend. Gratitude makes sense of our past, brings peace for today, and creates a vision for tomorrow.
— MELODY BEATTIE, *The Language of Letting Go*

* * * * * * * *

Taking the time to stabilize ourselves by doing the things that nurture our physical and emotional health is essential. Without that, we aren't in good shape to effectively care for ourselves or our kids, who are also dealing with our divorce transition. Becoming solid and grounded will go a long way toward having the attitude and perspective we need to support them and help them get stabilized.

You know why flight attendants, when giving emergency instructions, advise us to put on our oxygen masks first, right?

It's because if we pass out in an emergency, we can't help anybody else.

The same thing holds true with our self-care. If we don't take good care of ourselves — if we don't keep ourselves both physically and emotionally healthy, how will we care for our kids?

Our kids depend on us. And the best thing we can do for both our children and ourselves is to be in good running order. So it's important to do the things that keep us in top form so we can handle everything that comes our way.

How do we do that? Here are some things I've learned:

Do the little things, every day, that matter. Good daily decisions, done consistently over time, have an enormous impact on how we feel. It's these little things that may seem unimportant in the moment, that do matter eventually because they really affect our overall well-being. These things include deciding to:

- Eat healthy food
- Move your body every day
- Develop good sleeping habits
- Stay current with your health care appointments
- Nurture your mental health
- Watch your finances

Be grateful. When we're in the middle of our divorce, gratitude may be the last thing on our list. But gratitude is powerful. Making a decision to be grateful for your situation and your life can transform it into something entirely different.

Why? When we are grateful for something, we can't be resentful of it. Gratitude can move us from a feeling of scarcity to a feeling of abundance.

What are you grateful for? You'll realize there are tons of things once you start to tune in. It can be something that seems small, like:

- Flowers in your yard
- Food in your pantry
- Watching a good movie
- A phone call from a friend
- A delicious cup of coffee

Or something bigger, like:
- Living in the same city as your extended family
- Flexibility in your job so you can pick up your kids from school a few days each week
- Having somebody in your life who is encouraging you
- Living in a part of the world that experiences the beauty of seasons
- Your kids being healthy

What you are grateful for doesn't necessarily mean sticking to a particular formula. It can be anything that's meaningful to you.

Try keeping a journal to record what you are grateful for each day. Don't use the same things from day to day—choose new ones. Get yourself a journal and write down three or four things every day. The simple act of doing this trains your brain to look for the positive things in your life. As you'll soon discover, there are a lot of things to be grateful for.

Recognize when you've hit your limit and need to take a break. In the self-help/12-step world, there is a saying known as HALT. This acronym reminds us to not let ourselves get too Hungry, Angry, Lonely or Tired. The way to do that is to pay attention to what's going on inside of us—essentially, to be able to monitor ourselves so we know if we are on the verge of behaving in a way we know won't end well. For some people, these behaviors might be drinking too much or spending too much money.

Part of being a well-functioning person and parent is to pay attention to those signals when they happen and practice acting with loving responsibility toward ourselves so we model that skill for our kids.

Take comfort in the simple things in life. Many simple things you enjoy don't cost a dime. If you are tight on money, it's important to remember that many of the best things don't cost anything. What are your absolute favorite things to hear, watch, see, and do? Maybe things like:

- Snuggling with your kids while reading bedtime stories
- Cheering for your son or daughter's sports team
- Tending your plants and garden
- Talking on the phone with a sister or a friend
- A long soak in a hot bath with a good book
- A nap
- Lingering in a bookstore

Remember, these simple things are the important parts of your life. They are easy to do. They enhance your mood and your life. And they are free.

Find a positive distraction. With changes to your life and your schedule with your kids, you may have time on your hands that you are not accustomed to having. And with all these adjustments, you may be feeling a little blue.

Sooner or later you may have cleaned out every closet and organized every old photo. And if you have, don't sit idle waiting for life to come to you.

Support groups suggest volunteering in service of others as a way to pull yourself out of a funk. If you are feeling sorry for yourself and struggling to maintain perspective on your situation, find a way to help out people whose life situation is different than yours — specifically, people who are significantly disadvantaged, aging, sick, or need help. Essentially, find a positive distraction for yourself. Give some of your time and energy to an organization or agency that can benefit from what you have to offer the world.

- If you love to read, consider volunteering to read books to kids at the local library.
- If cooking is your passion, try cooking meals at a local homeless shelter.
- Do you have a musical gift? Can you sing or play a musical instrument? Maybe you can perform for seniors at a nursing home.
- If caring for animals is your thing, contact your local rescue shelter and see how you can help.

Being of service to others will give you insight that you may not have right now, and will help you focus on somebody or something other than yourself.

Keep your emotional energy clean. We are responsible for our mood and for the emotional energy we bring into a room. We've likely all experienced the situation where somebody comes into a room in a foul mood, and brings the energy of the room down immediately. It's even worse if you are someone who has tremendous influence on the other people in the room, like a parent, who has the responsibility of setting the example for your kids.

Kids are like sponges; they absorb whatever emotional energy is present in a room. If there is shame, blame, criticism, or other tension present, they'll take it all in. Then they pack it up in their subconscious memory and carry it forward with them into their adult lives. Is that what you want for them?

It's important that we keep our emotional energy clean. Remember, our kids may not seem like they are paying attention to what we do and say, but they are. How they emotionally respond to things is learned from us. Keep yourself as emotionally healthy as possible. Not just for the sake of your children, but for your own sake as well.

Now that you know how to take good care of yourself, you are ready to tackle the next component of stabilizing your life, which is to create a new routine for yourself and your kids. The next chapter guides you through how to do that.

ACTION ITEM

What things can you do every day that will help your physical and emotional health? Can you improve your eating and exercise habits so you have more energy and patience? Can you carve out ten minutes of quiet time just to think? Spend an hour outdoors? Read a good book? Make a list of the top three ways you can nurture your emotional and physical self.

CHAPTER 6

Create a New Routine

The key is not to prioritize what's on your schedule, but to schedule your priorities.
— STEPHEN COVEY

* * * * * * * *

As a young adult, I struggled to plan my days and schedule my time so that I could fit in all the things I needed to do. Thankfully, during that time, I had a friend named Kim who was an excellent role model for me. She got up every day at four o'clock in the morning. Because Kim was such an early riser, she got a lot of things done before the rest of us were even awake.

Kim's early rising habit made for an efficient use of her time in the morning, which was extra important when she was going through her divorce. During that time she had custody of her children 100 percent of the time, so she had a lot of things to fit into her day.

She would get up, do a load of laundry, make school lunches, plan the family dinner, pay some bills and still be at the gym for her morning workout when it opened at six o'clock. Her younger brother was between jobs at the time, so he moved in with her during that period so he could be home with her kids in the early morning.

Kim was amazing and inspiring. I was single at the time, and found it hard to drag myself out of bed and get to the gym—and I hadn't done anything before getting there. But she was creative with how she managed her daily routine and made it work for her situation.

Of course, with all that early rising, Kim went to bed early at night. But that didn't matter. Her kids were young, so she just went to bed when they did.

I learned a lot from Kim about how to plan my day and structure my time and schedule. I also learned that it didn't matter what time of day I got things done—I just needed to plan it all out and make it work for me.

* * * * * * * *

Your schedule will most likely change as a result of your divorce. The custody schedule you have, your working hours, and possibly even living in a different house will all make things different. Creating a new routine—one that suits what's currently happening in your life—is an important part of getting some stability for yourself and your kids.

A new, thought-out, defined routine will help everybody. The kids will know what to expect (Where will they be? Who is picking them up from practice?), and it will eliminate confusion for them. You'll know when you have time to get things done and you'll be able to maximize your efficiency when your kids aren't with you.

If you don't create a new routine, life can become chaotic. You won't plan time to get all the things done that you need to do, and you may run late for pickups. And if you're running ragged, you risk missing out on the sweet things that happen with your child.

After your separation, your average day and weekly schedule might be a lot different. You might have your kids part time. Or maybe you'll have them weekdays and not weekends, or maybe they'll be with you for alternating weeks.

Whatever the case, give careful thought to how you want to structure your routine now that your schedule is different. Do whatever feels right and suits your family's new schedule, because chances are, as a newly single parent, you'll be handling most of these responsibilities on your own, or with very little help.

Here are a few things to consider:

Change the way it's been done up until now. Part of being a single parent is that now there is just one (adult) vote on when to do things in your household. Of course, you have your kids' needs to consider, but if anything about your schedule when you were married drove you nuts, now you can change it!

Throw out the old ways of doing things and start thinking about innovative ways to restructure your daily schedule. Make up new rules about who does what. And get your kids to help in age-appropriate ways. Here are some ideas:

- **Create a schedule to share school drop-offs and pick-ups so you don't have to do it every day.** You probably have friends with kids the same age as yours — likely right in your neighborhood or building. Set up a carpool schedule whenever possible, so you aren't doing all the driving.

- **Break down your household chores into tasks and assign them to each family member,** based on their age and ability (things like washing dishes, folding clothes, assembling ingredients for tomorrow's lunches, etc.) Rotate the tasks on a regular schedule and adjust this as your kids can do more.

- **Change the order of when you do things.** Household chores don't have to be done in the evening or on the weekends. School lunches don't have to be assembled after dinner. Are you an early bird? Then do those things in the morning. Throw in a load of laundry or pay some bills before you leave for work in the morning, like Kim. Get some things done before you wake up the kids for school. It feels great to knock things off your list when the day is young.

- **Multi-task when waiting for kids at sports practices or lessons.** Set up a portable office in your car. Get an organizing caddy and stock it with the things you might need, like pens, tape, scissors, and cell phone and laptop chargers. My friend Mimi has done this for years. She's a teacher, so rather than make multiple trips back and forth from her home to her daughters' lessons, she grades papers while she is waiting for them. She also does everything from wrapping birthday presents to preparing holiday cards for mailing. It is a great time—and gas—saver!

Get things done when your kids aren't around. When sharing custody of your kids with your former spouse, there will be times when you are on your own, without them. That alone time may feel strange at first, but with time it will get easier. Those days and nights or weekends will start to become part of the rhythm of your new schedule.

Make those times work *for* you. Maximize the potential of those time blocks to get things done like grocery shopping and general errands, so it is easier when your kids are with you. Or use that time to do something special for yourself. Schedule alone time into the overall pattern of your life and create something that suits you perfectly.

Always allow more time than you think. As a single parent, especially of young children, you will likely have more things to do, places to go, and appointments to coordinate than you did when you were married. There will be a lot to pick up, move around, pack in a bag, and put in your car.

Make it easy for yourself—start early! It always takes longer than we think to get things done. When you are going someplace, put your stuff in the car well before you need to leave. Then leave early for wherever you are going. Allow yourself a fifteen minute time buffer. Inevitably, somebody's going to have to go back to the house to use the bathroom or pick up something they left. You may need to stop for gas. Traffic may be heavier than usual. Leaving early allows you to drive at a reasonable speed, which feels so much better—and is so much safer—than trying to make up for lost time on the road.

You won't regret leaving early. You'll arrive relaxed and ready to tackle whatever you need to do.

Cherish the time with your kids. Try to make peace with, and yes, even love the mundane things you do each day. Many activities need to be repeated over and over, like taking your kids to school, getting them to doctor appointments, making dinner and helping with homework, and it can feel like the monotony of those tasks drain the life out of you.

But remember — this is *it*. There is no part of this ordinary life stuff that is insignificant. These ordinary things *are* parenthood. They *are* the childhood your children are living. They *are* your kids' lives.

Like Gretchen Rubin (author of *The Happiness Project)* says in her video, *The Years Are Short,* "One day — and that day probably isn't too far away — you'll no longer be riding the bus together. So don't fritter the time away. Try to think of it this way — thank goodness, another day to ride the bus!" Because years later, it will be the simple, predictable, solid, repetitive things that your children remember and will have learned from — the everyday things that gave their life shape.

You will miss this stuff someday. Your children are only this age once. These are the good old days. Don't miss them while they are still happening.

When you have a routine or schedule that keeps life moving smoothly, feels good and works for your family, you will start to feel more grounded. As some of the schedule-related things will involve your former spouse, the value of a parenting agreement that spells out some of the specifics is significant.

In the next chapter, "Design a Parenting Agreement," I cover why having a parenting agreement is important, and some of the items to include in that agreement.

> **ACTION ITEM:**
>
> Given your new life, write out a plan for the best possible week you could have right now.
>
> After considering work and school, custody arrangements, and extra-curricular activities, how do you want to structure your day? What do you want weeknight evenings to be like? Who makes dinner? When does grocery shopping happen? How will you divide household responsibilities? You have an empty canvas—be creative about how you plan your daily routine.
>
> Both adults and kids usually do best with predictable and consistent schedules. How can you set up your new routine so you extract the most enjoyment and least frustration? Feel free to think way outside the box on this one!

CHAPTER 7

Design a Parenting Agreement

Start where you are. Use what you have. Do what you can.
— ARTHUR ASHE

* * * * * * * *

Consistency and predictability are essential to your kids' sense of stability, especially when their parents are going through a divorce. If behavior expectations, schedules, and rules are as similar as possible in the two homes where they live, it's easier for them to adjust.

Parenting children together after a divorce requires more than just co-scheduling time. Kids of divorced parents will do best if they have consistent rules and structures to follow. Take the time to create a parenting agreement for how you and your former spouse will work together to make it easier for everybody in the long run, and you will know how to handle all the situations that will come your way.

A parenting agreement is a written agreement between both parents that spells out how much time the kids spend with each of you, along with how decisions will be made about their care and education. It creates a consistent, detailed guideline to help you parent your kids together, during and after divorce. It means that you and your former spouse will need to mutually agree to focus on what is best for your kids.

There are a few things to consider when creating a parenting agreement:

- All of your children's needs are different; the needs of one may be very different from the needs of the others.

- It should be flexible. It is the basic structure you will use with your former spouse to parent your kids. There will always be exceptions.

- Neither parent is a winner or a loser with a parenting agreement. It is designed to make things as fair and equitable as possible, and to keep them that way.

- It should include a plan for handling disagreements.

- Consider getting an expert's help in working through the issues you can't resolve on your own.

The legal system has different suggestions for what should be included in a parenting agreement. You will likely be guided through these steps as part of your divorce process. If your parenting agreement doesn't cover the items listed below, please consider adding them:

- Custody schedule: Daily, holidays, vacation, school breaks, special occasions, changes to the parenting schedule, no-shift clause, first right of refusal for time with kids if you need to change the schedule

- Expenses: Who pays for what; which costs are shared

- Health: Medical, dental, vision care and appointments; administering medication

- Communication: Parent-to-parent, parent-to-child, contact with extended family

- Church/Synagogue/Temple: Attendance, religious study, social activities; especially if parents are of different faiths
- Transportation: Drop-offs and pick-ups, safety
- School: Attendance, school records, activities and functions, grades, after-school care, parent involvement
- Lessons: Music, dance, extra-curricular activities
- Sports: Teams, practices, out of town travel, game-days, tournaments, uniforms
- Child-care
- Child support payments
- Diet and exercise
- Personal hygiene and grooming
- Sexuality: Behavior, sex education
- Personal responsibility: Home chores, character, citizenship
- Sleeping arrangements
- Contact with parent's friends/dating partners
- Discipline/behavior consequences
- Movies/media: Parental controls, rating
- Driving privileges
- Internet and cell phone use rules, screen-time allotments
- Financial management: kids' bank accounts, allowance, spending guidelines
- Moving/relocation
- Anticipated changes to the parenting agreement (as children age)

- How to request/acknowledge messages to other parent and changes to child custody schedule
- How to handle disagreements between parents

Your divorce lawyer or mediator should help you create a parenting agreement that works for you and your unique situation.

If you prefer to create your own, here are a few great resources to check out. Visit BeckyAdams.net/parenting-agreement.

A parenting agreement won't ensure that you never disagree with your former spouse about something related to parenting your kids. But creating one, especially as a part of your divorce process, will help to clearly establish the guidelines you mutually agree are an important part of raising your children.

Finding a way to communicate well with your former spouse is a critical part of parenting together. In the next chapter, I describe how to create a pattern of communication that builds more stability.

ACTION ITEM:

Are there any special factors involved in the parenting of your children (special health or behavior issues, unusual parent schedule, etc.)? Consider what those may be and create a parenting agreement that covers your unique situation.

Be willing to ask the hard questions about how you will parent together as part of your divorce process. Don't put off dealing with these questions because you feel uncomfortable asking them right now. Getting a clear understanding and agreement now will help you avoid disagreements and misunderstandings later.

CHAPTER 8

Develop a Communication Plan

*The single biggest problem in communication
is the illusion that it has taken place.*
— GEORGE BERNARD SHAW

* * * * * * * *

My daughter's favorite music artist was coming to our city. She'd waited forever for him to schedule a concert in our area, and I was so excited for her. I wanted to surprise her by getting tickets for her birthday so she could go to the concert with a friend who also loved the same artist.

The day came to purchase the tickets and I scored two great seats in the first row of the balcony. Perfect! But I completely forgot to mention it to her dad. The concert was the kind of thing we'd previously agreed to check with each other about before giving her permission to attend. It was months away and it just fell off my radar as something to talk to him about—an honest mistake on my part.

The concert was scheduled for a date when my daughter was scheduled to be with him for the night. When I called to ask for a schedule change, he asked why. When I told him about the concert, he questioned whether or not it was appropriate for her to go to that particular concert without a parent.

Hmmm. That was a judgment call; one I thought I was okay with until we talked about it in more detail. I had to agree, it *would* be better for a parent to go. But there were only two tickets. And it would be heartbreaking for my daughter to not take her friend to the concert.

So, what to do? The solution to the problem cost me dearly— like hundreds of dollars dearly. I bought another ticket—at scalper's prices—so I could go to the concert with them, providing the parental supervision that was fitting for the event.

It would have been so much easier—and a lot less expensive—for me to talk to my former spouse about it in the first place. Lesson learned; remember to always check in when it comes to stuff like that.

* * * * * * * *

During and after your divorce, there will be lots of times when you'll need to communicate with your former spouse and your kids when they aren't with you. Developing a plan for how to do both of these things will contribute hugely to your sense of stability. You'll be able to reach your former spouse when you need to, which means you'll have the information to act and make decisions, and you'll have peace of mind knowing your kids are okay. Without a communication plan, you'll be left wondering when you can next connect, and that can feel pretty upsetting.

There are two important parts to communicating—first, with your former spouse, and second, with your kids:

Communicating with your former spouse: You'll need to communicate about a lot of significant things related to your kids: their schedule, requests for changes to their schedule, to coordinate pick-ups and drop-offs, to update each other on the results of doctor appointments, homework assignments, and to discuss what's happening with them in general.

This may be tough to do when you first divorce, when hurt feelings and raw emotions can affect how you feel like treating your former spouse, but give it a try for the sake and welfare of your children.

If you're able to have an amicable conversation, a brief chat at the pick-up or drop-off time will work. But if tension and anxiety levels are running high, and you can't communicate without getting upset in front of your kids, you'll need to figure out a way to get the job done without intensifying the situation.

Phone calls, email, and texting are all forms of communication that don't require a face-to-face conversation. Putting a notebook in the kids' back-and-forth bag (I describe this in the "Coordinate Efficient Drop-Offs and Pick-Ups" chapter) is another easy way to communicate with each other. You can leave messages and transmit forms or other paperwork that need signatures or that must be sent back and forth between houses. The details of how to acknowledge and reply to requests and messages can be decided in your parenting agreement.

If communication between you and your former spouse is working well, consider setting a regular (monthly, if possible) meeting or phone call so you can talk about upcoming events, the schedule, shared expenses and the kids' general well-being. If that kind of communication isn't yet possible, create a log or keep a shared file online where you can notify each other on a regular basis about what's going on in your kids' world.

Communicating with your kids: Moms sometimes experience intense anxiety about being apart from their kids, especially when they are first divorced, and custody schedules are new. Because of this, knowing how to reach your child and understanding when you can talk to them will greatly contribute to your sense of well-being.

Depending on their ages, they may have cell phones, which will allow you to stay in touch with them. If that's the case, then staying in regular contact won't likely be an issue. If your child is too young for a cell phone or doesn't have one and your custody schedule requires you to be apart for extended periods of time, try to set up a regular time to talk with them (this can also be addressed in your parenting agreement). It might be daily or every few days or every week; whatever works best. Just knowing when you can talk to your kids will ease the anxiety you may feel about being apart.

Try to agree in advance on certain things. Even though you are responsible for decisions made on behalf of your kids while they're in your care, there may be certain things you know your former spouse is sensitive to, which might cause you to second guess your decisions. So it makes sense to get input from him, and to agree mutually how to handle those predictable things *before* they happen.

Agreeing in advance is especially important when it comes to things like how to handle medical issues, allowable TV shows and movies to watch, and rite-of-passage things like ear piercing and dating. If you expect that any of these subjects may cause a disagreement between you and your former spouse, take the time to talk about them before they happen. Some of these things can also be addressed in your parenting agreement, if you have one.

And here's a super-important step: if and when you and your former spouse do agree on how to handle something, document the decision and note the date the conversation took place. Because later on, after the fact, you'll have something to refer to if you forget what your agreement was and when it happened.

Update, update, update. Depending on your custody schedule, it may be a long time between when your kids are with you and when they are with your former spouse, and a lot can happen in that period of time. Ongoing updates to him about what's been happening and things he should be aware of can make your kids' transition between homes go a lot more smoothly.

Remember, the kids are the ones who do the shuttling back and forth between homes. Make it easier for them by keeping your former spouse updated on what's going on with school work and projects, invitations for birthday parties and sleep-overs, friend problems, health concerns and the results of doctor appointments, as well as how they are doing in general. This is key to creating consistency for them.

When in doubt about whether or not your former spouse would want to know about something, *update him* has been the position I've taken. It takes a lot of communication to do it consistently, and sometimes I've forgotten and not done it. But updating pays off. The continuity it creates for our kids is worth the time it takes.

Communication with your former spouse is an important thing to get right, both for your own sanity and because it contributes significantly to your kids' sense of security. In the next chapter, you will find more ways to help your kids get stabilized as they move with you through your divorce process.

ACTION ITEM:

Draft an "Update" email template to your former spouse so you have it handy when you need to bring him up to speed on what's been happening with your kids. Here's a basic outline:

Hi _____,

Here are a couple of updates I wanted to share with you about _____:

Item #1

Item #2

Item #3

Please let me know if you have any questions or if you'd like to talk more about this.

Your Name

CHAPTER 9

Help Your Kids Get Stabilized

We want to shield our kids from the grief and the
pain they are experiencing. But at some point,
we have to let them heal on their own.
— CARI VOLLMER

● ● ● ● ● ● ● ●

The night we moved out of our family home, I tucked my daughter into bed in our new home—an apartment close to her school. She was very sad. She told me she hadn't gotten to say goodbye to our home. Even though she was only in elementary school, and it was nearly nine o'clock on a school night, we hopped in the car right then and drove back to our old place.

We went through the house room by room, talked about the wonderful times and memories we had there, and then said goodbye. It was sad and difficult to do, but in the end it seemed like there was some sense of closure for her. Because the transition out of our family home was a big adjustment for my daughter, it was important to handle it in a way that honored how she felt about it.

She wanted to maintain ties to the old neighborhood, so whenever possible, I kept her daily routine the same. One way that helped me do that was to continue driving both her and her best friend to school each day, just like we did when we lived next door to him. For the next two school years, we still went by and picked him up every morning, and he rode to school with us.

It was part of our routine and something my daughter looked forward to every day. She didn't want it to change. And it was one way for her to feel some measure of familiarity and control over her life while she experienced a lot of change all at once.

* * * * * * * *

Your kids will need your help in getting emotionally stabilized during your divorce. Helping them and teaching them how to do that is a loving, caring parental thing you can do for them right now. It will give them a place to voice the pain they are feeling. And that will allow healing and adjustment for them. Plus, you'll teach them that they can rely on you.

Without your grounding presence or a solid parental model in place to grab onto for emotional support, your kids may flounder and feel adrift. And because they are young and not may not be mature enough to verbalize what that feels like to them, it could manifest itself as anger, confusion, and feelings you probably don't want them to experience.

The new reality for your kids is that they are being raised in two homes. That will automatically mean they live in and experience two different home cultures as a part of the regular pattern of their lives.

I know how I feel when I go on a trip and stay in a hotel. I get settled in, and then a few days later, pack everything up and move on. Then I arrive home and unpack and settle in again. It's a little bit disruptive even to me, an adult with decades of experience, and I travel quite often, so I adjust quickly.

Imagine how it would feel to do that every few days, or every week? To sleep in different beds, have different toys and clothes, eat on a different schedule and follow different rules? If they split their time between two homes, that's what your kids experience.

Though you and your former spouse were once married to each other and shared the same home, there is likely a big difference in how your homes feel now that you live apart. Be gentle with your kids as they navigate the differences between their two homes. They are adjusting to two new sets of everything, and it will take some time for them to settle in and feel normal — their new normal — about their lives.

There are a few things you can do to make this process easier for your kids:

Maintain as much consistency for them as possible. Most people, especially kids, need consistency and predictability in order to function well. The divorce process can do a pretty good job of shaking that up for your family. So during that transition, do the things that create stability for your kids. Is eating out on Friday nights at a favorite restaurant something that your kids look forward to doing? Do you make blueberry pancakes every Sunday morning? Can you keep driving them to school, like I did with my daughter? Whatever it is that creates consistency — keep doing *that*.

Give them a sense of control of their circumstances. What kind of leeway can be built into their schedules and lives? Where can they have some input into decisions that give them a sense of control over their lives? Find that place and let them have it.

Encourage them to talk about it. I saw a television interview with David and Francine Wheeler, parents of Ben Wheeler, who was tragically killed in the Sandy Hook Elementary School shooting in December 2012. They described how they were helping their son Nate cope with the loss of his younger brother. An important part of Nate's healing is to be free to talk whenever needs to — about Ben or whatever else he needs to talk about — and to be encouraged to keep talking.

The same encouragement is important for kids during and following their parents' divorce. Too often, even though they are stuck smack in the middle of it, the divorce subject is taboo. They aren't allowed to voice their pain or talk about it at all. Parents are often in so much pain themselves, they forget to check in with their kids and see how they are doing. But kids need the chance to talk.

Allow them to talk about whatever they need to talk about. Encourage them to just say it and get it out. This will allow healing to happen.

Give them "stabilizers." Kids often struggle to adjust to living in two homes or living without one parent or the other. This is especially true if custody arrangements mean significantly more time with one parent than the children are used to having.

There are little things you can do to make the transition easier for them. One that works well for a young child is to tuck a surprise note into their pocket, jacket, or lunchbox.

Tell them you love them, you are thinking of them, or what you look forward to doing when you are next together. If your child can't read yet, draw him or her a picture that explains what you're saying.

Another thing you can do is give your child something special to hold in their pocket, or get him or her something special to wear—like a bracelet or necklace, so they can know and feel that you are thinking of them when you are apart.

I always put a special note in my daughter's bag when she goes away for extended periods of time. Some families use a secret hand squeeze or a special wave. Develop something that works perfectly for you and your kids.

Allow your child to heal on his or her own time. Realize and understand that it is your kids' experience that matters to them, not yours. Everything is relative to your kids. Even if you think they should be adjusting to your divorce within a certain period of time, they may not be. You can't manage or control how they feel. Instead, you need to allow them to heal in their own time.

Be physically and emotionally present for them. During your divorce, your kids' lives have likely been turned completely upside down. They may be confused, angry, and resentful of the recent changes in their lives. They may be feeling anxious about living in two homes—maybe two *new* homes. More than ever, they need to know and trust that, without a doubt, you will be there for them, both physically and emotionally.

Sometimes, in the turmoil of our lives, we fail to consider how our kids are feeling about all the changes going on.

We get so focused on all the things happening to us, that we neglect to have a plan to support them.

This *is* the time to consider their feelings. This *is* the time to listen to what they are telling you. This *is* the time to be a solid, stable presence for them. This *is* the time to create a comfortable and secure home environment.

Even though it may not seem like it, your kids are paying attention to what is going on. They are observing and absorbing what happens, how it happens, and how it feels when it happens. So it is vitally important that you are both physically and emotionally present for them.

How do you do that?

- **Keep your promises.** If you say you will be there, be there. Pick them up on time. Get them where they need to go on time. Be the person they can count on.

- **Have a solid backup plan for yourself.** Arrange for somebody to cover for you, so you have a backup plan if you are stuck in heavy traffic or unavoidably held up and can't get to them on time.

- **Be a role model for how to handle these tough times.** Your kids will know you are sad and probably struggling to get through this period of your life, but it's important for you to be a role model for them through this. It's just like in a barnyard or at the park—the little ducks follow the big ducks. What does that mean? It means that the big ducks teach so the little ducks can learn. You are the big duck, and you need to lead by example. In tough times—divorce, death and other family struggles — our kids' emotional responses will model ours. If they see we are holding it all together, they will do the same.

Part of helping our kids to get stabilized is asking for help from our community and the other people that influence them. In the next chapter, I describe the importance of getting help from your kids' teachers and the other important and supportive adults in their lives.

ACTION ITEM

Think about the areas of your kids' lives where you can create consistency with their old lives. What's one thing you can do right now that would provide an enhanced level of stability for each of your kids? Do that.

Feel free to use some of my suggestions or build your own stabilization tools to help your child navigate this important time of transition.

CHAPTER 10

Get Help from Your "Village"

Never doubt that a small group of thoughtful,
committed people can change the world.
Indeed, it is the only thing that ever has.
— MARGARET MEAD

* * * * * * * *

My divorce took place when my daughter was in elementary school. There was a parent-teacher conference scheduled within the first week of our separation. My former spouse and I were both very involved in our daughter's education and school life, so we both attended the conference. I told the teacher a few days earlier about our separation, so she was aware of our situation when we came to the meeting.

I remember that it felt weird to be there that day with my former spouse, so soon after we had separated, but it was for the benefit of our daughter, and so I wouldn't have missed it for the world. I trusted that these types of joint conferences would get easier with time. They did.

A few years later, that same teacher got divorced. I ran into her when I was out shopping one day, and she told me she was encouraged that day my former spouse and I showed up to the parent-teacher conference together, so soon after we had separated. She remembered the commitment she felt from us toward mutually supporting our daughter. It made a difference to the way she handled her divorce. She was inspired to do the same thing for her daughter.

* * * * * * * *

Teachers and other important adult caregivers are the "villagers" you need to raise your child. After all, it takes a village to do so, especially after a divorce. During the school year, your child often spends more hours each day with her teachers and other caregivers than she does with you.

Let your village know about the major changes taking place in your family so they'll understand your child's situation. That way, they can watch for unusual behavior, such as frustration, anger, or intense sadness. These kinds of behavior indicate that your child is struggling with the changes in her life, and they can keep you updated so you can take action to help.

Many schools have great resources to help kids through transitions like this. Guidance counselors are trained to listen to and watch kids carefully, and can give suggestions for how to cope with the anxiety they might be feeling.

In addition to the emotional support your child can get from teachers, coaches, program leaders, and caregivers, there's also great benefit to keeping these adults in the loop for practical and logistical reasons. For example, most school-related activities are designed for a child that lives in one home. When there are two homes, it becomes harder.

Depending on the day activities take place, and which parent the child is with on that particular night, two sets of permission slips may be needed, or a second set of instructions or textbooks. Then there's the night when your child leaves her homework at the other parent's house and can't access it before school. Having the teacher's understanding of the situation can help immensely!

There are lots of school-related activities where parental involvement is required. It will make your child's life a lot more peaceful if you and your former spouse can work together with your child's teacher to participate in activities like:

- Parent-teacher conferences
- Field trips
- Homework and special projects
- Volunteer, room parent, and Parent-Teacher Organization (PTO) activities
- Special pick-up requests

When you get the assistance of your kids' village, it can be of exponential help to your child. Their combined effort will make a big difference to the amount of support your child feels.

Enlisting the help of your village may feel like one more thing to add to your list, and one more group of people to talk to when you least feel like it. If that's the case, and you are struggling to do this, remember that all of these stabilization ideas are incremental. Some of them will happen slowly. Some of them may not happen at all.

Try making a little progress every day. You don't have to do everything all at once. In the next chapter, "Aim for Progress, Not Perfection," I describe the downside of trying to get everything perfect the first time around.

ACTION ITEM:

List all of the significant adults in your child's life right now. What can you communicate to them or ask of them to support your child through this transition?

CHAPTER 11

Aim for Progress, Not Perfection

You don't have to get it perfect; you just have to get it going.
— JACK CANFIELD

* * * * * * * *

I remember the day I sat looking at the paperwork I needed to do in connection with my divorce.

It felt overwhelming. I needed to compile a bunch of financial information and I didn't know where to gather it all from. I'd moved recently, and my personal financial records seemed to be scattered across a few boxes rather than all in one place.

But this task needed to be completed by the end of the week. So I decided to break the task down into small little pieces—things I could do easily in a ten-minute period. Over the course of a week, I'd have the job finished.

Day one: I'd find the boxes. Day two: Make a stack of the tax documents. Day three: Look through the documents to find the information I needed. Day four: Complete the forms. And just like that, I was finished. It wasn't perfect, and it didn't happen overnight, but I got it done.

* * * * * * * *

Do you find yourself immobilized sometimes? Not sure which direction to go next, or which task to undertake?

The list of things we have to do can seem endless and often overwhelming. Sometimes we feel like there is so much to do that we can't do any of it the right way. In the midst of that, it's easy to stop moving, or stop making forward progress. Or else we just start doing random stuff without any particular plan. The next thing we know, we're running around and not making much of a dent in our list of things to get done.

Get a plan together for what you need to do to accomplish little things, one at a time. Stitched together, these will contribute to some great progress and that will feel really good. That kind of forward movement adds to our overall sense of stability and self-confidence.

The goal is to make forward progress, not to get things done perfectly. Just keep moving. Break that big to-do list down into smaller pieces and tackle each task one by one.

In her book, *Daring Greatly,* Dr. Brené Brown talks about perfectionism and why it gets in the way of making progress. Reading it helped me enormously. I learned that perfectionism isn't about aiming for excellence or healthy goals. It isn't focused on improving ourselves and it doesn't promote success.

Instead, perfectionism—when we set crazy high standards for ourselves and try to do things flawlessly or please everybody—can cause anxiety and near-paralyzing procrastination. Then we don't get anything done. Perfectionism is actually a destructive behavior. It leaves no room for us to improve what we're doing, or the chance for much joy in accomplishing things. Instead, we're always focusing on what people think and being critical of ourselves and how we're doing things. This affects how we feel about ourselves and what we're able to accomplish.

But if we focus on making progress instead of on being perfect, we can move forward a little bit every day. This allows us to move in the direction we want to head, and to enjoy the journey and the progress we make along the way.

When this happens, we can appreciate a different kind of perfection: the kind that comes in the everyday, ordinary moments as simple surprises. These are those wonderful, unexpected times in life when things align just so — kids laughing, your favorite song on the radio, three green lights in a row and returning home together after a busy day. That's the kind of perfection I want to experience!

Adjusting our expectations of ourselves around the subject of progress, and being gentle with ourselves about what we can achieve is an important part of creating stability for ourselves. It is another lamp along the dark street that will guide us in the direction we want to go. This helps us practice treating ourselves in a way we want to be treated. And when we see ourselves making progress, it gives us the courage to change how we treat our former spouses. That's where we're headed now.

ACTION ITEM:

Are there areas in your life where your need to be perfect or to do something perfectly is holding you back from completing a task or being truly present with your child? What one action or next step can you take to move yourself forward?

CHAPTER 12

Practice the Golden Rule

*Words are very important things. They get into the
wallpaper, the carpet, the upholstery, our clothes—
and finally, ourselves. You must be very careful about
the words you use to describe yourself and others.*
— MAYA ANGELOU

*　*　*　*　*　*　*　*

Despite their decision to divorce, Chris and Shawn decided
to keep many of the promises they made to each other on their
wedding day. Even though the marriage part of their relationship was over, they still had two kids to parent together, which
meant ongoing interaction between the two of them.

Together they agreed to honor many of the original promises
they made to each other—like respect and honesty and to be
the best possible parents for their kids.

Things weren't always so amicable though.

When they first separated, Chris didn't agree that he should
pay child support to Shawn for their two kids. Shawn had been
a stay-at-home mom when they were married, and now that
she was working again she earned a lot less than Chris. Chris
wanted to go to court to settle their disagreement, but Shawn
didn't want to. She felt sure they could work it out themselves.
But she told him she'd go that route if he was certain that's
how he wanted to handle it.

Shawn's friends urged her otherwise. They thought she should definitely go to court. But Shawn stuck to her belief about Chris and their relationship as parents. She said, "I'm picking my battles. I want a relationship with this man. We have two kids to raise together. I know Chris, and I know how attached he is to his money. That's his security. If I go after his money, he and I will have nothing, absolutely nothing."

And she was right. Because Shawn was patient and understanding about what was important to Chris, it allowed him to come to terms with the child support payment requirement on his own time. Eventually, he agreed to pay a higher percentage of their kids' expenses than Shawn initially thought he would.

Now it is give and take between them. Sometimes Shawn gives Chris money and sometimes Chris gives Shawn money, depending on the situation. They've bent over backward to work together for the benefit of their kids—because they agreed to be respectful of, and honest with each other.

* * * * * * * *

Regardless of how it is now, what kind of relationship do you ultimately *want* to have with your former spouse? If you are raising your kids together, chances are you want it to be an honest give-and-take, and to have an agreement to put the kids' best interests first and to trust each other to do that.

In order to have that kind of relationship, you must set your behavioral standards high. Remember that words can hurt. Once spoken, you can't take them back. So, please— don't speak badly about your former spouse when your kids are around, no matter how tempting that is or how angry you might be. Remember, he is your children's other parent, and hearing that kind of thing is like poison to them. If you have something negative to say to him, do it privately when the kids aren't around. Or confide it to a close friend.

A judge in Family Court described it this way. He said to the parents, "Think about shooting an arrow through your ex-spouse, but it goes through your children first." That's what happens when you don't think about how your words affect your kids.

Creating a new relationship with your former spouse after your divorce can be an enormous challenge. So often, there are layers of hurt and disappointment that get in the way of useful communication. And assuming it was tough to get along when you were married, it'll likely get even harder after you divorce.

So assume from the start that it will take time and patience to get to a point with your former spouse where you can get along and work well together to parent your kids. And even then, you will not always agree on issues. In fact, you may rarely agree. See if you can start with a process that respects each other, and build from there.

A great piece of advice I got on this subject was from an old friend. During my divorce, she suggested that I should expect and envision my former husband and myself communicating in a way I knew we were both ultimately capable of doing. That expectation, in turn, would cause me to behave appropriately toward him.

In other words, in the midst of that sensitive, post-separation, raw-emotions time period when couples often treat each other badly because they are hurting—treat each other the way you know you are both capable of behaving, even if you don't feel like it yet. Move the behavior before your feelings get there. The good will and good habits created by doing this will set into motion a pattern of treating each other respectfully.

Really, it is just like the golden rule. Do unto him as you would have him do unto you.

Sometimes we need a little help to keep our own behavioral standards high. Moving past the pain or hurt of our divorce can be helped by performing a personal letting-go ceremony or ritual. In the next chapter, I tell you how to do that.

ACTION ITEM

Are there times when your interaction with your former spouse goes off the rails? Do you ever treat him badly in front of your kids or others?

What are the things that push your buttons the most? What can you do in advance to ensure you are prepared for those moments?

CHAPTER 13

Perform a Ceremony

*Holding on is believing that there's only a past;
letting go is knowing that there's a future.*
— DAPHNE ROSE KINGMA

* * * * * * * *

Angie and Rob performed a ceremony around their decision to divorce. After years of struggling, they mutually decided that it was time to end their marriage. Rather than take the usual course of dissolution that includes lawyers, fighting, and opposing positions, they decided to simply...let go.

They met for coffee one day and talked frankly about all the positive things that had come from their marriage to each other—their kids, experiences, and the places they had lived. They also talked about some of the things that hadn't gone well, and how those had hurt their relationship. But in the end, they knew it was time to part.

So they gave each other the gift of a ritualistic divorce. They released each other from the marriage commitment they had made to each other years before, so they were free to move on with their lives. Then they started the legal part of their divorce process.

* * * * * * * *

I love the idea of performing a ceremony or ritual to help ourselves make peace with something that's causing us pain or holding us back. Ceremonies can be powerful, transformative, and helpful for a variety of reasons: to let go of something we are holding onto emotionally, to forgive ourselves or somebody else, to move on from something, or even to celebrate something.

Without the benefit of rituals like this, sometimes we stay stuck where we are, holding onto things like regret or anger. This often gets in the way of our ability to move forward and create a happy new life for ourselves — a life free of behavior we don't want or emotional baggage we've been hauling around.

In 2012, I had the amazing experience of going to Paris with a group of women — a "retreat" kind of trip, where we had time to reflect on what was going on in our lives and to encourage each other to achieve our big dreams. One activity we did together was a ceremony of leaving behind something that no longer served us. We gathered at the Saint Sulpice fountain in central Paris, where we were each given a coin that represented what we were going to release. One by one, we approached the fountain and tossed the coin, at the same time letting go of whatever was holding us back.

It was a powerful experience, and one I will always remember. I still remember the decision I made that day and what I decided to leave behind at that fountain in Paris.

There are lots of reasons to perform a ceremony for yourself and an endless number of ways to do that. Try one of the following:

- Write a goodbye letter to somebody or something (with no intention of sending it), and then burn or shred it afterward.
- Perform a "letting go" ceremony, like Angie and Rob did in the story.
- Celebrate a decision to change something about your life.
- Visit a place that is sacred to you and mark a decision with a special activity while you are there.
- Mark a milestone or goal with a special event.

Whatever it is that you feel might benefit from a ceremony, I encourage you to do it. It may seem like a simple, silly thing to do that it wouldn't make any difference, but the impact can be truly significant.

ACTION ITEM

Is there something you need to let go of, accept, move away from, or celebrate? If so, create a ceremony that feels right and comfortable to you—one that helps you move toward feeling peaceful about a particular event, or to a point of acceptance about a new behavior or way of thinking.

In this section, *Get Stabilized,* we've covered a lot of great ideas to help you and your kids get stabilized throughout your divorce transition. Implementing these ideas will help you understand the specifics of what is happening during your divorce, get a handle on how to create a new schedule, and take care of yourself so you can help your kids get stabilized. In doing so, you'll be creating a strong and happy life for yourself and your kids. Yay you!

Now that you know about the things you can do to solidify your life during your divorce process, you are prepared to move to the next stage of the transition, which is to get organized in all areas of your life. The next section will lead you through several practical steps you can take to organize everything from your home, to your financial life, to how you coordinate drop-offs and pick-ups for your kids. There is a wealth of information that will create a feeling of empowerment and a feeling of, "Yes, I can do this!" in you.

2

Get Organized

CHAPTER 14

Practical Things

Organization isn't about perfection. It's about efficiency, reducing stress and clutter, saving time and money, and improving your overall quality of life.
— CHRISTINA SCALISE

* * * * * * *

The steps up to my second-floor apartment looked twice as long as normal. Ugh, and there was that gross smell again. My downstairs neighbors seemed capable of cooking the world's worst smelling food. Every single day.

I hated grocery shopping on the best of days, but today, hauling the bags across a parking lot and up a flight of stairs, I felt especially miserable. I missed the garage in my old place that had easy access to the kitchen.

Following the sale of our family home, I wasn't quite ready to buy a place on my own yet. I needed to scout out the options available, and as much as possible, get the perfect place. So I chose to move into an apartment close to my daughter's school. It was convenient to all the things that were familiar to us, and because of that there were fewer changes to incorporate into our lives. But this apartment, with its tiny rooms and zero storage space, was going to be a challenge for organized living—even though this was only intended as a temporary housing situation.

I did the best I could to set up our little apartment so it worked as well as it could for us. And I got a hand cart to make the trip from the parking lot with groceries a lot easier.

Having a comfortable and organized place to live was important to me. I felt like it was one of the starting points for creating my new life that felt peaceful and not chaotic. And with all the changes that had been going on in my life lately, I wanted my home to feel good.

I've always been an organizer. That comes easy to me. But what I learned during my divorce, especially with a kid involved, is how much *more* organized I need to be. And not just related to my home, but also my schedule, my paperwork, and yes—even how I shopped for groceries.

• • • • • • • •

Getting your life organized, by taking time to do things like laying out your calendar for the year, setting up your home so it functions really well for you and your kids, and planning great meals, is one of the nicest things you can do for yourself as a single parent.

When things are organized to suit your life, it means you will have time to get things done, your kids' lives will be more peaceful and predictable (which means less stress for all of you!), and you'll have a feeling of contentment because unexpected surprises will be minimal.

Not taking the time to get your life organized paints quite a different picture. You'll be running from one thing to the next, constantly running late, unable to find things, overdrawing your bank account, and living a frazzled life with your kids.

In this section, *Get Organized,* I lay out a detailed plan to help you get your life organized. Because I'm an organizer by nature, this is my favorite section. If you follow the advice in these chapters, your life will smooth out, and you'll feel deeply empowered. These suggestions are a whole new set of streetlights to brighten that street you've been walking down. And by the end of the section, you'll have the information you need to get truly organized so life feels great for both you and your kids.

ACTION ITEM:

What areas of your life feel disorganized or are in a state of chaos? Consider these as you read through this section. Open yourself to the ideas presented, choose the pieces and parts that resonate with you, and then act on them.

CHAPTER 15

Set Up a Calendaring System

*Go confidently in the direction of your dreams
and live the life you've always imagined.*
— HENRY DAVID THOREAU

* * * * * * *

Even a rock-solid calendaring system can get screwed up.

I had my super-detailed calendar. I filled in all the dates for known events at the beginning of the year, and I updated it on a regular basis. But once I forgot to add something. In this case, it was to note a schedule change my former spouse had asked for a week earlier, which meant I forgot to pick up my daughter from soccer practice one day — completely forgot. She called me on her coach's cell phone — a call I almost didn't answer because I didn't recognize the number.

"Mom?" she said. "Where are you? Are you coming?"

I immediately had that terrible feeling in my stomach — the one that's reserved specifically for when you screw up and forget to pick up your child. And this screw up was a dilly. It wasn't the coach's phone she was calling on — it was the phone belonging to the director of the entire recreational league her team was a part of. Yep, he was filling in for her coach that day, and I'd kept him waiting for almost an hour with my daughter while I was, well…not coming.

My daughter hadn't been concerned at first that I wasn't there, because I don't typically forget stuff like this. She thought it was unusual, but figured maybe I was just running five minutes late. But then five minutes turned into ten, and then fifteen, and then thirty. At that point, she got worried. The combination of the sound of her worried voice on the phone and my realization that I'd completely forgotten to pick her up—that hit me like a ton of bricks.

I pretty much broke all the posted speed limits on my way to get her that day. And when I arrived and tried to explain to the director that, "Really, I'm not usually late," he just looked at me. Obviously, he had places to be.

Because it wasn't my regular day to pick my daughter up from soccer, and because I forgot to note the change on my calendar, I was happily working away, completely oblivious to the fact that I needed to go and get her.

Big fat lesson learned. Note any change to your schedule on your calendar as soon as you agree to it!

* * * * * * * *

The first step in getting yourself organized is setting up a family calendar so you can track everybody's activities. When you get a reliable calendaring system in place, you can be so much more proactive about schedule-related things.

You'll know the days you need to call in reinforcements for things you can't do on your own. It will prevent those moments of panic and wondering, "What am I going to do?" that happen when unanticipated things come up. Lay out your calendar early in the year to give yourself peace of mind. You'll have an overview of the whole year, so you'll know what's coming and be prepared.

You'll need a dependable system for recording all your family's activities. There are lots of them to choose from. Online versions can make it easy to share information between households. You can check some of these out at BeckyAdams.net/calendaring-systems.

Or you can use the plain, old tried-and-true paper version — or a combination of both. That's what I've found to be the most effective. An online calendaring system makes it easy to access your information from anywhere, but there's also something cool about using a paper version. There's just something about having a hard-copy record of what you've done all year that just feels right to me.

My favorite paper calendar is the More Time Moms Family Organizer® (moretimemoms.com). I've used it for many years. I love looking back at it to see what I was doing at the same time in prior years. It's great to see the progress I've made and remember the fun times I've had with my daughter. It creates such a great permanent record of our lives. Whichever you decide to use, make sure it can support all the things that need to be scheduled and recorded.

There are lots of things to consider:

Custody/days spent in each home: If your custody schedule is fixed, the information will be easy to record and duplicate on your calendaring system. If, on the other hand, it is somewhat flexible and dependent on your schedule and the schedule of your former spouse, then it will take a little more time to document and will require frequent updating. It is also important to note traded dates and to document any situations where your custody agreement breaks down or is not properly adhered to, such as late (or missed altogether!) pickups.

School schedules: Check your school district's website for a list of dates that schools are closed. Be sure to record not just legal holidays, but also back-to-school nights, winter and spring break weeks, weeks with half or shortened days (for parent/teacher conferences or teacher planning days), sports-related activities, plays and performances, teacher recognition days, achievement ceremonies, open house dates, dances, graduations, and any other dates specific to your area and school districts.

Sports, practices/lessons, extra-curricular activities: If you and your children are involved in sports and activities, there will be a lot of information to record on your calendar. Note practice days, game days, performance days, travel weekends, and special-study periods.

Birthdays: Record your children's birthdays, your birthday, and the birthdays of any family members or friends you want to remember and celebrate.

Holidays: Record all holidays (legal, statutory, religious, etc.) that you observe. Make sure you remember Mother's Day!

Vacations: Do you take an annual trip with family members or friends? Is there a week you spend at the beach every summer? Or a ski trip each winter? Record any and all likely vacation dates. Does your former spouse attend a regular conference or sporting event the same time each year? Is there a guys' trip (ski, golf, etc.) that's part of his yearly schedule? If so, see if you can arrange your vacation or part of your vacation with the kids during that period. That way, you can take advantage of double the vacation time—both his and yours. And, you won't need to make a special request in order to do it!

Family events and reunions: Some families spend time together each year or celebrate an annual event together on the same weekend. Record those special dates as well.

Doctor/dentist appointments: It's easy to let a year (or two!) slip by and forget to make annual appointments for your children's regular checkups—doctor, dental, vision, etc. Schedule these kinds of appointments well in advance, and be sure to record them on your master calendar.

Summer vacation and camps: Do your children attend the same camp each summer? Do they spend a week at Grandma and Grandpa's place?

Work-related travel: There are a couple of industry-specific conferences I like to attend each year. They typically occur during the same week. This is the case with many professions. Are there training, education, or ongoing certification sessions you participate in each year?

Special anniversaries of the heart: What days are special to you? Are there special days you observe each year? A day in honor of the loss of a loved one? Or opening day for your favorite sports team? Is there an annual no-school day you allow for your kids? Everybody has dates that are special to them. Make a place for them on your calendar so you can work them into your schedule. They are the events that form the memories that last all year.

After all the important dates are recorded, take note of whether or not they occur on your custody days, or on days when you already have things planned. If so, will you need to make different child care arrangements on those days? Will you need a backup plan so your son can be picked up from sports practice? It's likely you'll discover a lot of scheduling issues as you record your scheduled activities for the year. Your early-calendaring system will make it all so much easier to manage.

Now that you have the information you need to set up an efficient system to calendar all your activities, you are ready to move on to the next step of getting organized, which is giving thought to where you live. The next chapter covers the things to consider related to your neighborhood so you can make a choice about where to live that feels good to your whole family.

ACTION ITEM:

The ongoing maintenance of your master calendar is an important part of feeling organized and on top of your schedule. If you don't have a master calendar already, get one today. Take the time to record important dates for the rest of this year. Record everything you are aware of right now, and add to it as the year progresses.

CHAPTER 16

Give Thought to Where You Live

*The doors we open and close each
day decide the lives we live.*
— FLORA WHITTEMORE

• • • • • • • •

After my divorce and the sale of our family home, I needed to make a decision about where to live permanently. We'd moved into an apartment complex as a temporary living solution while I was looking for a place to buy. Because my daughter was firmly rooted in the school in our neighborhood, and we had lots of friends in the area, I wanted to stay as close as possible to our old home.

But buying a new place to live in that area was a bit of a challenge, as this was a financial stretch for me. Most housing in the area consisted of single-family homes priced higher than I could afford.

So I went to work on solving the problem. Sticking strictly to my defined budget, I narrowed down the options I had for where to live. It turned out that there were only two options in the area—two different condo developments that were completely different from each other, but were places I could afford. Having just two options for where to live made it a lot easier. I was able to be focused in my search, and quickly make a decision.

I purchased a condo that was the perfect size for my daughter and me. It met all of my criteria; it was within walking distance of all the schools she'd be attending between elementary school and high school, a short commute for me to work, close to friends and our support system, and there was easy access to shopping and restaurants. It kept our lives simple and uncomplicated, which made this an easy decision.

* * * * * * * *

Living in an area that is convenient for your new life is the next step in getting organized. When you live in an area that suits your lifestyle, this eliminates all kinds of hassles from your day-to-day life. It means easy access to work, schools, food, and the other conveniences that make life so much less frustrating. I'm all for making life easier whenever possible.

If you have a choice about where you will be living, consider these things before making your decision:

Proximity to your kids' schools. This is a huge factor. Living close to school will make your life so much easier. I feel so strongly about this that I suggest — when in doubt about your options — choose the location closest to the schools. This allows for easier drop-off and pick-up, is less stressful when it comes to attending school events, and possibly even allows kids to walk to and from school. (This is big!) As a single parent, time is precious, and this factor alone will save you many headaches and white-knuckle trips home from work — trying to navigate traffic to arrive in time to pick up your kids.

If at all possible, use your home address rather than your former spouse's address, as the address of record for your children in your school district. While most notices are typically sent via email rather than U.S. mail, some information is still distributed the old-fashioned way. If yours is the address of record, you will be sure to get this information, and you won't have to rely on the school's system for sending duplicate copies of this information.

Easy access to work. Live as close as possible to where you work. You may not have control over this, but if you do, choose quick access to work! There are many advantages: short commute time (which equates to hours saved), low gas costs, the possibility of eating lunch at home (which equates to dollars saved), and the ability to get home quickly when necessary. This is especially important on the days when you have a sick teenager staying home alone or when you're in chauffeur mode, getting kids to after school activities, lessons, and practices.

Access to grocery stores, gas stations, and restaurants. Let's face it — taking care of the daily-business-of-living chores consumes an enormous amount of time. Living in close proximity to the stores and services you use on a weekly basis really helps. It makes a quick trip to the grocery store to pick up a forgotten ingredient for tonight's dinner a lot easier, and if you can combine that with a stop at the pharmacy and then pick up the occasional take-out dinner — all the better! Choose easy whenever possible.

Stay close to what's important. What matters here is that you are close to whatever is most important to you. That could be your parents and siblings, or maybe close friends who are a critical part of your support system. Or the ice rink. Or the yoga studio. If you have a choice, make the one that best suits your needs, and that will help you support your family's lives and schedule.

Choosing the right area to live is super important. The next step after that will be to create a new home for yourself and your kids. In the next chapter, I take a closer look at how to set up and organize your new home, so it feels good and works well for you.

> **ACTION ITEM:**
> What are the things or places that are important for you to live close to? Do you need to have a single family home rather than an apartment? Would a second-floor apartment provide you with better security than a ground floor unit? Do you need a yard or is there a park in the neighborhood that is a reasonable substitute? Make a list of what's important to you and use it as your personal checklist for where to live.

CHAPTER 17

Create Your New Home

Home is the nicest word there is.
— LAURA INGALLS WILDER

• • • • • • • •

Having a home that is organized and works well for you is a critical aspect of organizing your life. When you do, you can make the most of the space you have, and this is especially helpful if you've moved to a smaller home. It also makes the care, maintenance, and cleaning of your home a lot easier to manage, and that's something that will help you a lot as a single parent.

Failure to get your home organized will create its own set of problems. You could end up buying or renting a place that's the wrong size for you and is tough to maintain. You may feel like your home is constantly in chaos, or just doesn't feel right.

Following your separation or divorce, it's possible your living arrangements will change. If you stay in the family home and your former spouse moves out, there will likely be a division of furniture and household things that make the space feel different. If you move to a new place, you'll be dealing with an entirely new space, possibly smaller than the one you had before. Whatever the case, take the time to set it up so it works well for and feels good to you.

Make the space work well. As a single parent, you may be juggling more things on your own than when you were married, so getting your home in order so it works well for you is key. Having an organized space will be a huge time and frustration saver, and you'll likely need all the help you can get right now.

If you are moving to a smaller space than you are accustomed to living in, you may not be able to keep all of your furniture. Or you may be moving to a new place and, because of your recent division of household items, you may not have enough — or the right pieces of — furniture to adequately furnish your new home.

If that's the case, get creative! Things don't have to be set up in a traditional way. Can some rooms serve a dual purpose? Is it possible for some of your furniture to be repurposed? Do whatever it takes to make your new home feel warm and familiar.

Here are a few things to consider as you organize your home.

What spaces/areas do you need?

Sleeping: Regardless of your child custody arrangements — full time versus shared — if possible, be sure the new home you choose has a separate bedroom for your kids. They need to feel they have a place of their own, where they belong. If your former spouse stays in the family home and you are the one that moves out, this is even more important. In this case, you are establishing a second home for your kids, and it's important that it feels stable and permanent. Sleeping in the living room on a pull-out sofa or a camp cot in your bedroom won't give them the feeling they are longing for. Having their own space is essential; otherwise things may feel temporary, and their sense of home will align solely with the other parent's home.

Living room: Is there a place for your family to sit together and watch your favorite television show? Or play a board game? What activities are most likely to take place in the living room? How much seating do you need?

Kitchen /dining room: How much room do you need in the kitchen? Do you cook dinner every night? Is there an eating area in the kitchen? Or is there a separate dining room?

Home office/homework: It is important to have a designated area to deal with schedule-related things and paperwork related to custody, support, shared expenses, etc. Also, in order to do homework, kids need a quiet study and reading area.

Laundry/utility/mud room: Does your home have laundry facilities or an area to hang-dry clothes? Can you install a hanging rod for drying clothes over the washer and dryer? Can you create a drop zone for shoes and backpacks by installing a bench with hooks above? Can you section off part of your coat closet for storing your vacuum and brooms?

Garage/storage: Do you have enough space in your garage to park your car? Or is the entire space used for storage? Is there a place in your home to store things like bikes and kids' outdoor toys?

Should you rent a storage unit for the seasonal items you rarely use so that you can free up other areas? It may be easier and less expensive than to rent or buy a larger home. Do the math to figure it out.

Are there areas that can be used differently than what they were originally designed for? After my divorce, I bought a small two-bedroom condo for my daughter and me. The size was perfect when I purchased it. A few years later though, after I started working from home and needed a home office, the space no longer worked as well. So I decided to change the way I used it.

The living room became my office. The dining room became our living room, and we got a smaller dining room table and moved it into the kitchen. I had to switch out a light fixture so the living room suited its new purpose, but the cost and effort were minimal — much less than moving or buying a new place.

It felt a little bit weird at first, but with a few well-placed bookshelves to act as room dividers, and a clear understanding of how I wanted it to function, it worked really well.

This is an area where you can get creative. Do whatever it takes to make your home work for your unique situation.

Find a logical place for everything. If you have to move the holiday decorations every time you dig out a sleeping bag so your son can go on a sleepover, that doesn't work! You'll function best if you have your home organized so everything has a place. And that is more than just buying storage bins and pretty baskets for your stuff. It means seriously thinking about the things you have, the things you honestly use, the things you can get rid of, and then finding the right place for what's left.

If this kind of process isn't your thing, enlist the help of an organized friend to lead you through the project. It takes a little time, but the end result is so worth it.

Put together a home tool kit and resource manual. Your tool kit should include basic things like a hammer, screwdrivers, pliers, a wrench, a level, a measuring tape, an assortment of nails and picture-hanging hardware, spackle (for patching those tiny holes when you put the picture in the wrong place), and touch-up paint.

Your resource manual should record light bulb sizes and wattages, refrigerator water filter number, furnace and A/C filter sizes, and anything else you need a record of, along with phone numbers and contact names of key people at your Home Owner's Association, your landlord or management company, security alarm contact, plumber, and electrician. Go to BeckyAdams.net/tool-guide for more information.

Learn how to be handy. This may not seem glamorous, but it will save you tons of money over time. If you don't know how already, learn how to:
- Replace light bulbs
- Change furnace filters
- Unclog a drain/toilet
- Turn off the water, power, and gas to your home
- Use a drill/electric screwdriver

Make your new home feel good. Pay attention to how your home *feels*. You've had a lot of changes in your life recently, so take the time to make it feel like an authentic reflection of you and your kids. When you do, your home will feel more inviting, warm, and familiar, which helps to create a feeling not only of organization, but also ongoing stabilization and healing.

For you: Focus on what you *have,* not what you don't have anymore. If the amount of household items and other stuff you have now is significantly less than before, make it all count. Surround yourself with the things you enjoy most and that appeal to your senses.

What do you need to have around you? What do you need to do for your home to feel homey? Do fresh flowers in a special vase lift your spirits? Can you use your grandma's quilt as a throw on your sofa? Find the things that bring you the greatest sense of comfort and place them front and center.

For your kids: Make sure your kids have the personal items they need to feel at home in their new space. If some of their things (clothes, toys, books, etc.) were divided up in the separation process, be sure that some of their familiar, favorite things are incorporated into their new surroundings.

For older kids, it may be fun to integrate some of those things into their new bedrooms or to let them update the look of their rooms. For younger kids, be sure to bring stuffed animals, favorite photos, and toys. Do everything possible to make their transition to a new home as comfortable as possible.

Create a blessing for your home. When I moved after my divorce, I wanted my home to feel like a safe haven and sacred space. I wanted it to be a place I was happy to come home to — where I could relax, heal, and recharge myself. I wanted to create a blessing for my new home, so I could give it the specific feeling I wanted.

Based on that, a dear friend wrote this blessing for me and read it at my housewarming party, in the company of my close friends.

"A Blessing for This Home"

Today, within this home a new chapter begins
Sure to infuse these walls with a new story.
So we celebrate with those we love and hold dear,
A warming ritual — a blessing for this home
And our expectant wishes for those who now live here.

May this home resonate with love which is practiced,
Not merely as words uttered but in actions fully expressed.
May this be a house brimming with laughter, joy and fun
Where wonderful, lasting memories originate and take shape.

Let this be a space where it's okay to cry and be real;
To be honest and transparent. Free from fear.
A safe harbor, a soft place to fall, rich with tranquil grace.

Where acceptance, forgiveness and encouragement,
Learning and gratitude have opportunity to flourish.
Where tangible peace is present and anxiety is released.

A home furnished with color, music, books, and art.
Quilts and projects. Floors full of toys. Candles for burning.

Old pictures and fluffy pillows and warm, fuzzy things.
Mementos and tokens of life passionately lived.

Perfect cappuccinos and plentiful wine.
Burgers burnt on the grill when conversation got in the way.
Friends who've become family circled round the table
Telling stories, relishing the moments, and sharing hope.

In this home, this house, this place, may all who enter
Or simply knock on the door in passing, experience
The uncommon spirit that is present and resides here.

When you have a home that is set up so it works for you—so it feels good and you're happy to come home to it—this will contribute a great deal to your overall feeling of organization. It will feel good to be in control of how your home functions and works.

Having your finances in order is also something that will contribute enormously to feeling organized and in control. In the next chapter, I'll show you what to focus on, to get—and stay—on top of your finances.

ACTION ITEM:

By blessing my new home, I started out with the positive, peaceful energy I wanted to feel while living there. Every person is trying to create something different for her home. What kind of blessing would be meaningful to you for your new or changed home? Make a list of the things that would make your home feel special and write out a sample blessing for your home.

CHAPTER 18

Get on Top of Your Finances

*Nothing you can purchase feels as satisfying
as financial independence.*
— MANISHA THAKOR

• • • • • • •

A friend who was going through a divorce confided to me that she was unsure of her financial situation. She knew how much money was coming in, but she'd never taken the time to figure out exactly how much she was spending each month, and how much debt she had. Because of my divorce, I had gone through the process of getting clear on all aspects of my financial life a short time before this, so I was in a good position to help.

The first thing I helped her to do was list everything she owed—every single credit card, charge card, and line of credit. This was a critical step. Until she understood how much money she owed, she was in no position to make any other decision about how she spent money, or to put together a plan to pay off the debt.

The result of the list was a huge surprise to her. She had far more debt than she realized. But she felt a lot better knowing the specifics of how much she owed, rather than living in a state of constant wondering. After that, she was able to plan a way to pay off the debt. It took her over three years to get rid of it all, but now she's debt free and clearly understands her financial situation.

* * * * * * * *

Being in control of your money and knowing how much you have is powerful. When you control your money, you have choices. And I want you to have as many choices about your life as possible, so be sure you know how to manage your money.

If you are feeling overwhelmed by the idea of managing the finances for your family because you've never done it before, that's okay. You can do it. This chapter will give you all the information you need. Here's how to get started:

Get clear on your financial obligations. In the "Know the Details of Your Situation" chapter of this book, I provided a list of things to know related to your finances. Be sure you understand what you are responsible for, and how and if your financial situation will change once you are divorced.

Know your numbers. It is critical to know, in detail, exactly how much money you have coming in each month or year, and how much money is going out. Just like when you manage a business, you must understand whether or not you have the money you need to cover all of your expenses. This is also called a cash flow statement. Take the time to determine and record these things:

- **Income:** How much money do you have coming in—from all sources? Include the amount you earn personally, plus any money you will be receiving in the form of child support or spousal support. Also include any investment payouts, family assistance, or money from any other source that you will receive each month or year.

- **Expenses:** How much money is going out? What are all of your expenses? Be sure to include expenses that are paid quarterly, annually, or seasonally. Find out exactly when automatic payments are withdrawn and what they are for. If you had a joint account with your former spouse, are there any payments that you have carried over to your account that should now be terminated?

Create a budget and stick to it. Along with clearly understanding what your income and expenses are, it is important to create and use a budget to manage your money. This is especially important if money is tight for you. If you aren't using a budget and you overspend, this could cause all kinds of anxiety and stress for you. The fees and penalties for overdrawing your account can add up quickly and create an even bigger problem. On the other hand, managing your money effectively leads to a sense of security and peace of mind that nothing can replace.

Live within your means. If at all possible, figure out how to live on what you earn by yourself. Make decisions about the home you can afford to rent or buy—and your expenses in general—based on how much money you make alone, and not by including the child support or spousal support that you may be granted through the court system.

That way, if things change for your former spouse and as a result, your child support or spousal support amount is changed or eliminated — your financial stability won't be affected. That may mean you need to opt for something smaller and more modest than you've been accustomed to living in, but the peace of mind will outweigh the stress of wondering if the support will continue.

Get rid of unnecessary expenses. Do a careful audit of your accounts and get rid of any expenses for things you no longer need, and research items you don't recognize. It's easy to forget about the things you pay for on a monthly basis that continue to charge even if you aren't using them anymore.

Have a cushion. Following your divorce, if you have some money from the sale of your family home or an equalizing payment of some sort, consider keeping it as a financial safety net versus spending it. The sense of ease you will have as a result will likely be worth a lot more than the joy you will get from whatever you might spend the money on.

If you don't already have a savings account safety net, start to build one as soon as you can. There is tremendous freedom that comes from having a cushion of money to cover unexpected expenses. It eliminates all kinds of unnecessary worry about things like whether or not your child support payments will be made on time and whether or not you will be able to pay the rent.

And there may be times when you'll need to front the money for an expense that you and your former spouse will eventually share, such as school trips, sports-related expenses, and medical bills. Having a little money set aside to cover those things makes life a lot easier.

Get help for what you don't know. After your divorce, you may need to learn how to "stretch a buck," and work within a budget to keep your family and household operating in the black. If the whole subject of financial management is like Greek to you, educate yourself. Take courses at a community college, consult a financial planner, take an online course, or ask a trusted friend for help. Be sure to ask somebody who is knowledgeable and disciplined with their money.

Get legal help if you need it. Sometimes divorce puts people in a fragile financial place. The result of some divorces is that there is just not enough money to cover expenses, or the debt cannot be managed. If that's the situation you are in, and you are considering bankruptcy, be sure to get legal help early on, so you can get to work on rebuilding your financial life as quickly as possible.

In a lot of cases, money-related issues contribute to the breakdown of marriages. If this was the case for you, it's extra-important for you to give this topic careful consideration — for your sake and for the sake of your kids, who are learning how to manage money by watching you.

Being proactive, knowing your numbers, creating a budget, living within your means, having a safety net, and getting help for what you need to learn are all vitally important steps to ensuring your own financial peace of mind and to feeling organized. In the next chapter, "Square Up Shared Expenses," I cover how to even up the costs you and your former spouse have agreed to share related to your kids' expenses so that it's easy and hassle-free.

> **ACTION ITEM:**
>
> Create a spreadsheet to record exactly how much money is coming in every month, and how much is going out. Does your income exceed your expenses? Create a budget so you know how much money you have available to spend. Do this as early as possible after your divorce, so you don't unknowingly get in over your head.
>
> Go to BeckyAdams.net/cash-flow-spreadsheet to download a sample worksheet.

CHAPTER 19

Square Up Shared Expenses

*If you don't know where your money is going,
you don't know where you are going.*
—ANONYMOUS

* * * * * * * *

There are usually quite a few kids' expenses that parents decide to share as part of their divorce agreement. And while the decision to share the expenses is one accomplishment, the payment of and reimbursement to each other for those expenses can be an ongoing challenge. It requires that you keep your spending records up-to-date and the payments to each other current. What you'll want to aim for with the squaring up of expenses is an equitable way of paying for your kids' expenses, and then reimbursing each other on a regular basis.

The benefit of squaring up consistently is that you'll stay current with reimbursing each other for whatever you may have spent, and one person won't be fronting the cost for an unreasonable period of time. The downside of not evening up consistently is that, unless you keep really detailed records of what you've spent, it is easy to forget and end up paying for a lot more things than you may need to. This is a particular problem when finances are tight and there isn't much of a cushion to front the money while you are waiting to be paid back.

I'm sure it is no surprise to you that the ongoing job of raising your kids costs a lot of money. Your divorce agreement with your former spouse should outline the basics about who pays for what related to the kids' expenses, and then how other child-related expenses will be shared between the two of you.

Since it's impossible to anticipate all the child-related expenses you'll need to share with your former spouse, think about adding them to your parenting agreement (described in the *Get Stabilized* section) if you miss some obvious ones in your divorce agreement.

Here are some ideas to help keep this task from growing too big:

Keep good records. Create an expense journal or spreadsheet to track all of the things you pay for personally that need to be shared between you and your former spouse. This is important because there are lots of expenses associated with raising children, and you won't have receipts for all of them.

Good record-keeping is the key to managing this task. Consider this the business side of being a parent. As I explain in the "A Plan for Paperwork" chapter, copying or scanning receipts, documents, and invoices is necessary when it comes to documenting what you have spent. You can visit BeckyAdams.net/expense-journal for a sample expense journal.

Know who pays for what. As I explained in the chapter titled "Know the Details of Your Situation," make sure you have a clear understanding of who is responsible for paying what. You may have the big things like education and medical care worked out, but what are you doing with smaller things like cell phone bills and soccer shoes?

Mutual agreement can go a long way with these general types of expenses. To keep it clear though, if you and your former spouse mutually agree that one of you will pay for something for your kids, make a note of the conversation in your expense journal. Note what the expense is and the date of your conversation. Also include any notes about why you may be paying the expense (such as "former spouse was out of town,") or why this may be a unique or one-time type of expense.

If your former spouse is the person paying for a certain expense and will be expecting you to reimburse him for a portion of it, it's important for you to have that cost noted in your budget. Otherwise, you may not set aside enough money to cover your part of the expense when it is time for you to pay it.

Schedule a regular meeting to settle up shared expenses. Ideally, this will consist of each of you comparing your expense journals with each other. You can compare the expenses and reimburse each other according to your agreement. The frequency of these meetings is up to you, but I suggest once every six months at a minimum. Every quarter (three months) is better, and if you have a lot of expenses, it may be necessary to compare and square up every month.

The meeting doesn't need to be in person. You can send each other your expense records and then have a quick phone call to discuss. A word of caution; don't give original expense documents or receipts to your former spouse. If they get lost, you will have nothing to document what you've spent. Always keep the originals yourself and send a copy to him.

For the regular, ongoing shared expenses that can only be paid by one parent at a time, consider trading time blocks. For example, school lunches can be purchased in most schools by setting up a prepaid account for your child. Try sharing the expense by funding the account for the first semester of school and then switching off for the second semester of school. That way, no reimbursement must take place; you can each simply pay the school directly for half the year.

It is important to have your paperwork in order so that you can be confident about the accuracy of the information you are sharing with your former spouse related to your kids' expenses. This allows you to document and back up your requests. The next chapter gives you great tips on how to achieve that sense of organization regarding all of your paperwork so you can effectively manage all the papers and documents it takes to run your life.

ACTION ITEM:

Go back to your divorce agreement and make a spreadsheet of the child-related expenses you have agreed to share with your former spouse. List how often the expense occurs and who is paying for it. Make sure you have added the expense into your own budget figures so you have set aside the money to pay for your portion when the time comes.

You can see a sample expense journal worksheet at BeckyAdams.net/expense-journal.

CHAPTER 20

Create a Plan for Paperwork

Paperwork wouldn't be so bad if it weren't
for all the paper. And the work.
— DARYNDA JONES

· · · · · · · ·

Paperwork can feel like it is taking over every horizontal surface in our homes. In fact, part of being a functioning person seems to involve an endless flow of paperwork. Sometimes, the hardest part of managing this is getting started on the job of wrangling it under control. There are a lot of things to manage and coordinate in your life, and often, paperwork—while critically important—is the last thing on your to-do list.

At least that's the way I used to feel. Then I had a great "A-ha!" moment about it.

A friend suggested I change the way I viewed my snarled mess of paperwork and the related burden I felt it all caused. Instead of considering it an insurmountable task, maybe I could come at it from a completely different angle.

"What task is easy for you?" he asked. "What happens in your home that you never think about, almost like you are on autopilot?" The answer was easy: the laundry. I love doing the laundry. I never think about it. It just happens. A load goes in the washer. A load goes in the dryer. It gets folded. And I start over. And even though it never ends, I don't view it as insurmountable. I have a great system in place to just keep getting it done.

"So what if you could view your paperwork the same way?" he asked. "What if you could figure out a way to create a system so it was handled, and you didn't have to stress about it?"

That made sense to me, so I decided to change how I tackled the job of managing all my paperwork.

First, I started to open all mail as soon as I got it. The junk immediately went into the recycle bin. The bills and other things requiring action were placed on my laptop keyboard. I immediately inputted them to my banking system for payment, filed them, or acted on what I could at that moment. Anything else was put in a small pile, and addressed at an appointed time; every Sunday night I spent a few minutes cleaning up loose ends.

It took a few months to come up with the plan that worked best for me and for it to all become a habit. But now it's a no-brainer. It happens just like the laundry.

*   *   *   *   *   *   *   *

Even though the world is largely digital, the ongoing and daily business of living still requires that we process and manage a lot of paperwork. If you have a place to collect it, process it, act on it and file it, the paper management side of your life will be a *lot* easier.

Add a divorce to the equation, and you have a recipe for a huge paper blizzard in your home if you don't stay on top of managing it all. Divorces create a lot of paperwork; things you need to act on in a timely way or file away for future use.

If you put a system in place early on to keep track of all the paperwork it takes to run your life, you'll be glad you did. It will eliminate the frantic digging through boxes of files and searching through your storage closet for tax returns and other documents you need. With a great paperwork management system in place, a weight will be lifted from your shoulders, your space will be clean and clear, and your mind will be free to do the stuff you really like to do!

Here's how to get started:

Set up an area in your home and on your computer. Set up a specific area of your home and designate it as your home office. If you don't have a separate room or part of a room available for this, create a corner office nook for yourself and furnish it with a desk, shelves, and filing cabinet — or whatever you need to accommodate all your papers. And do the same with your computer. Make sure you have a file structure set up so you can easily and quickly access the paperwork you need to use on a regular basis.

Plus, dealing with custody-related matters and the ongoing trail of paperwork that is necessary to raise a child means that a specific place needs to be established for this important paperwork. It will save time when you need to find something quickly.

Create a plan for organization and a place to file things. Mental clutter from looking at piles of paperwork and unfinished tasks weighs heavily — maybe a lot heavier than the unfinished task deserves. Set up a filing system for all of your paperwork needs. When you put a plan in place for how and where paperwork is organized and filed, it's a lot easier to keep things moving and get them completed.

There are many things to consider when setting up your system. You'll need separate folders for things like:

- **Financial documents:** Tax returns, bank and investment statements, mortgage and loan documents, paid bills

- **Divorce/child custody documents:** Your divorce settlement agreement, child custody agreements, and schedule

- **Child-related documents:** School registration forms, permission slips, sports and camp forms, shared contact information for daycare, after school care, teachers, doctors, lessons and practices, and the ongoing paperwork needs that go along with raising kids

- **Medical documents:** Contact information for doctors, immunization records

- **Insurance:** Policy and beneficiary information

- **Home maintenance and repair:** Contact information for your landlord, general contractor, electrician, plumber, and handyman

- **Other:** Birth certificates, adoption paperwork, passport information (be sure to record the expiration date on your calendar!)

And then do a similar thing with your computer. Set up a similar structure to file and save the digital version of the documents listed above.

Maintain paper records of critical things. Life creates a lot of paperwork. It may be tempting to go paperless for all your records, but there are still some things for which you should keep a physical record because they are so import- ant. Digital records work great for most things, but if you can't access them for some reason, there is no substitute for having a paper hard copy.

What things should you keep a hard copy of? This is an area where a lot of people's opinion differs, but for me this includes tax returns, mortgage and loan documents, and year-end statements, as well as all your divorce-related paper- work and estate planning documents. If these are currently in a digital format only, print them out and put them in your folder system, so you have a permanent paper record.

Get the office equipment you need. The ongoing task of maintaining an organized paperwork life is a lot easier if you set get the equipment you need to do the job well from the very beginning.

There will be times when you'll need to give your former spouse a copy of something that relates to your kids. So if you don't already have one, invest in a home printer/ copier/scanner. This may seem like an obvious thing, but I've noticed that a lot of people don't have one. It will allow you to document or duplicate all of those important things that should be printed, copied, or scanned — like drug prescriptions, school and camp forms, membership cards, and homework items — without having to go out to the closest copy center to do it.

Be sure to keep a supply of extra ink/toner cartridges, as well as extra reams of paper so you always have what you need. In the single-parent household, it seems like paperwork projects often happen late at night, when office supply stores are closed. Having extras on hand will save you from a frustrating night.

Shred everything you don't keep. In the world of rampant identity theft, be sure to shred all documents containing financial or personal data. Don't just toss them into the trash can or recycling bin and put them out with the week's trash. Instead, either take them someplace where you can have them securely destroyed or shredded, or invest in a home shredder and do the job yourself.

If you struggle to stay on top of your paperwork, you can use the same approach I did to change my view on it. What is an easy task for you? Do you love to cook so, for you, cooking isn't a chore? Are you disciplined about working out? Do you always send birthday cards to your family and friends? All of those things require a process that you must complete, so you keep doing them. The management of your paperwork works the same way.

Getting your paperwork in order is a critical part of being organized, and one that will leave you feeling inspired to keep up this habit. The next step on the path to organization is coordinating efficient drop-offs and pick-ups of your kids to and from your former spouse's home. In the next chapter, I give some tips on how to make that easier.

ACTION ITEM:

If you don't have a good paperwork management system working for you, give some thought to how it would work best. Everybody's needs are different. Design a filing system to catch all the regular paperwork you deal with on a weekly and monthly basis.

For a sample document planning system, go to BeckyAdams.net/paperwork-management, where you can download a structure that will work for most households. Then mirror your physical and digital filing systems so the folders in your file cabinet are the same as the folders on your computer.

CHAPTER 21

Coordinate Efficient Drop-Offs and Pick-Ups

Life's journey is one big path with a series of events. All these events are connected.
— LAILAH GIFTY AKITA

* * * * * * * *

If your kids share their time between two homes, drop-offs and pick-ups will be an ongoing, regular part of your life. It is helpful, then, to be organized about how you handle them so they go smoothly—every time.

Have a good plan to ensure that the transfer of stuff happens without forgetting things and that the drop-offs and pick-ups happen on time. Continually forgetting things means extra trips back and forth between homes, and that just gets old after a while.

Here are ways to make drops-offs and pick-ups a *lot* easier for yourself:

Shuttling stuff back and forth. Even if you have duplicate setups for your kids in both homes for things like clothing, toys, electronics, school materials and personal care items, there are always a few things that need to go back and forth with them.

The *things* will change over the years, but the need for them to go back and forth will remain constant.

When kids are little, there may be a favorite stuffed animal, toy, or blanket; or there might be specialized medical equipment or prescription drugs, books being read, and school work or projects in various stages of completion.

To save yourself endless frustration and to keep it all straight, come up with a fail-proof system for moving these things back and forth. Here are some things that worked for me:

- **Identify a special bag for the job.** Use the same one, week in and week out. And give it a name. Choose something obvious like the "red bag." That way, there will never be any misunderstanding of which bag you are referring to. Make sure it's big enough to carry their essential things and small enough to transport easily.

- **Clean out and check the contents of the special bag right away.** As soon as possible after your kids arrive back at your home, clean out their special bag. It almost always contains something that needs to be washed, or something tossed in at the last minute from their other home, on its way back to you. I know I've misplaced some of my daughter's clothing for weeks because I didn't check her special bag often enough.

- **When not in use, store the essential, absolutely-MUST-go-back-and-forth items IN the bag.** Things like emergency medications, special toys and study materials—whatever items your child can't live without.

- **Create an indestructible checklist (laminate if necessary!) for the important, but *not* critical items that go back and forth between houses.** On this list, include things like sports uniforms and equipment, special toiletry items, favorite shoes, lunch boxes, books, and the like. Confirm the items on the checklist are in the bag before you zip it up and hand it over.

- **Designate a drop-off location for the special bag in case you are not home.** In order to provide easy transfer of your child's stuff if you are not home to receive it, get a bench or trunk with a lockable storage area and put it on your front porch, back porch, side yard, or any place that is accessible by your former spouse if you aren't there. Get two keys, so you can both access it. That way, there is a safe place for the bag to be dropped off, and it is protected from the weather until you get home.

- **When your child's age/grade requires it, buy a laptop computer for them to use for their schoolwork and be sure it goes back and forth in the special bag.** That way, they will always have access to whatever files they need, without the complication of a different computer brand, file type, etc. to hassle with. Believe me, one late night spent trying to figure out how to make versions of a software program compatible with a different computer, and you'll be grateful you bought it.

- **Buy duplicates if you need to.** Even though the cost was double, I decided to get two sets of orthodontic retainers for my daughter—one set for our home, and another for her dad's place. That decision alone has probably saved dozens of evening trips between our home and his, and kept her retainer-use schedule on track. There may be other items like that in your child's life. Sometimes it's worth biting the bullet and paying the money for those extra things.

- **Label *everything* that belongs in your home.** As soon as you get something new for your child, label it in a way that makes it easy to understand it belongs in your home. This is the only way you will remember what belongs where.

You might remember the big things, but it is the little things that will kill you—those freezer packs that go in lunch boxes (it feels like I've bought hundreds of them over the years!), socks, underwear, and even clothes. After a while, it all starts to look the same, and you won't be able to remember where it belongs unless it's labeled. Do yourself a favor and make friends with a Sharpie® Laundry marker. It will become your new BFF.

- **Keep an inventory of what you've purchased.** When you buy clothes for your kids, chances are they are for a specific event (even just for school) and you'd like to have them available for wearing when they're with you, right? Keep track of them by making a written or even a mental list, so you can remember what they have. Then, if those clothes are taken to your child's other home for a special occasion and they don't come back right away, you can ask for them to be sent back so you aren't stuck buying replacement clothes at the last minute when you have a special occasion pop up. It is frustrating—and a real wallet-drainer—when you have to buy clothes to replace ones left in the other home.

- **Make a mental note of what your child wears when she goes to her other home.** If you do this, you can check to make sure the clothes come back to you again. If you don't, it is really easy to lose track of them. This is especially important with seasonal clothes you don't use as often (winter coats, hats, and gloves, etc.) and special occasion items like dress shoes and jackets.

- **Agree on a way to notify the other parent if one of you is running late.** Call, email, text—whatever you mutually agree works best—be sure to keep the other parent in the loop. If your child is being picked up from your home, have her special bag, school backpack, and other things ready to go and placed by the door. The other parent may have rushed to get there in order to be on time, so be respectful of their time by having the kids and their things ready to go.

- **Make sure your kids are fed, clean and rested.** Hungry, dirty kids aren't typically very pleasant to be around—and it makes their transition to the other parent's house a lot tougher. The same goes for being tired. Well-rested kids can manage the change easier than over-tired, grumpy ones.

- **Verbally confirm the next step or transition point at each interaction.** Even if your custody schedule is set in stone and drop-offs/pick-ups take place as planned, it is still a good idea to confirm the next transition point at each interaction. A quick "See you on Friday morning" or "Have a good weekend together; see you on Sunday night at seven" keeps everybody on the same page. Plus, continual, ongoing confirmation of the schedule is helpful because sometimes it jogs the other parent's memory of a schedule change they've been forgetting to request.

- **Allow yourself a time buffer.** Don't schedule any appointments, meetings, or social engagements just before or after pick-up time. If a delay occurs, you'll be late. Allow yourself a time buffer of thirty minutes to an hour so you can get where you are going on time.

- **Hold the sensitive conversation for later.** Don't discuss issues and problems—like whether or not you've received your expense reimbursement payment—in front of the kids at drop-off/pick-up times. Communicate those sensitive things privately to each other via phone, email, or text.

Once you have the drop-offs and pick-ups down pat, you can move on to organizing other areas of your life. And the next thing is…food! Planning ahead for what to buy, cook, and eat takes a huge weight off your shoulders when you are a one-parent show. In the next chapter, "Plan Ahead for

Dinner," I talk about the importance of organizing how you handle weeknight dinners and food at your house.

ACTION ITEM:

Get out your Sharpie® marker and start labeling! Put your kids' initials or some other identifying mark in an inconspicuous place on their clothes, toys, electronics and anything else of theirs. Obviously things like socks and underwear will be hard to label, but try to find a place on everything else.

It is tough enough to keep all your kids' things accounted for when they live in one house; when that increases to two homes, the confusion doubles. Make it easy for yourself. Label everything you can.

CHAPTER 22

Plan Ahead for Dinner

Cooking well doesn't mean cooking fancy.
— JULIA CHILD

* * * * * * * *

My friend Ann is a fitness and healthy lifestyle coach. When her clients complain about feeling overweight and unhealthy, she asks them, "Do you know what you're having for dinner?" Her belief is that if you don't know what you are having for dinner—if you haven't planned for it, and you are in a hurry to get dinner on the table—then you are an accident waiting to happen.

And by accident, I mean, there is a great likelihood that you'll end up eating something unhealthy and spend too much money doing it.

> Lack of planning for dinner
> + rushed circumstances
> = dinner disaster

* * * * * * * *

With more and more national focus on eating healthy food as a way to optimize your health and wellness, the importance of getting organized about what you feed yourself and your kids is becoming more critical every day. And there's no place where this is truer than in a single parent situation.

When there is just one of you to pick up the kids and then bring them home and make dinner, the importance of *planning* healthy dinners for your family becomes super important.

Pre-planned, healthy weeknight dinners make the whole week go better. Kids are fed before they are starving. You have a chance to eat together and talk about your day and what's going on in your lives. Homework can be started on time. Bath time can occur as planned. And on and on. It's like a magic wand for a peaceful evening.

We all know the reality of *not* planning because we've all experienced it—lots of times. You get home with the kids. They're hungry. You're tired. Everybody wants to eat right now. You want something simple, quick, and healthy. Simple and quick trump healthy right away, so you reach for a frozen pizza—or a box of macaroni and cheese from your pantry. Or worse yet, you pick up fast food on the way home. And you end up feeding yourself and your kids an unhealthy meal.

What if that could be different?

Let's rewind a minute. How about spending a few minutes on the weekend—before the work and school week starts—to plan out your family dinners for the week? Precook some chicken, chop some vegetables, plan some crockpot meals, and do anything else possible to make your weeknight meals easier for yourself. At the very least, defrost what you plan to cook the next night.

In order to make your food/dinner planning a lot easier, think about these things:

What basic staples do you need in your house? What things should you never run out of? When you have your kitchen stocked with the kind of healthy things that your family enjoys and you eat regularly, you have lots options for what to make. It's kind of like mix-and-match cooking. You can grab that pre-cooked chicken, add some rice and a bag of frozen vegetables, and you'll have dinner in less than a half hour. There are an unlimited number of combinations and options if you plan ahead and have some of the basics already on hand.

What are the essential items to have for your kids? Peanut butter, cheese, apples, baby carrots? And for you? A favorite soup, salad fixings, chocolate?

In my house, the things we *can't* run out of are packages of frozen brown rice, chicken breasts, eggs, frozen fruit for smoothies, ice cream, and coffee!

Here are some great ways to make weekday dinners run smoothly:

Do batch cooking. It is so wonderful to come home at the end of the day and have dinner almost ready to eat. When you do batch cooking—cooking large batches of food, and either refrigerating or freezing it for future use—you can do that. It's great. With a short heat-up time (usually about ten minutes), you can have dinner on the table.

This has become one of my favorite ways to handle weeknight dinners. I get whatever vegetables are in season, cook or roast them in large batches, vacuum seal them in bags, and freeze them for use later on. I do the same with chicken and meat. It makes dinner so easy and is a *huge* time saver.

Keep a running grocery list. Put a list up on the refrigerator of the things you need to buy at the grocery store. Ask your kids to help you keep it updated with the things you need to buy on the next trip. Keep doing this until it's a habit for everybody in your house to note an item as soon as it runs out.

For a list of planning resources and information on batch cooking, you can visit BeckyAdams.net/plan-ahead-for-dinner.

Taking the time to plan, cook, and eat healthy meals is a win-win all around. It is a great gift you can give yourself. You won't believe the difference it makes in how your week goes and how organized you feel. And it makes a huge difference to the health of your family, too.

We all live busy lives, and keeping up with our family's health care needs and regular checkups and appointments must be a priority if we are to stay healthy and active. In the next chapter, "Manage Your Family's Health," I give you the tools you need to keep yourself and your kids in top form.

ACTION ITEM:

Make a customized grocery list for your family. List all the things that are staples in your home—the things you should never run out of. Chances are you'll be buying those things on every shopping trip anyway, so you might as well have a list that is mostly complete before you even start. Print it out and fill in the rest before you go shopping for food. It will save time for both your meal planning and your shopping!

You can download a sample list at BeckyAdams.net/grocery-list.

CHAPTER 23

Manage Your Family's Health

Take care of your body. It's the only place you have to live.
—JIM ROHN

• • • • • • • •

Shortly after my former spouse and I separated, I was at home with my daughter early one weekend morning. We'd been watching Saturday morning cartoons in bed. I stood up to go to the bathroom and was immediately seized by a terrible back spasm. I'd never felt anything like it before in my life. I don't know what triggered it, but the pain was intense. I could not walk, but instead had to lay down flat on the floor.

My daughter, who was only about seven at the time, was scared because I was completely immobilized—unable to sit or stand or walk. After lying there for about half an hour, hoping the pain would subside, I realized it wasn't going away any time soon, and that I'd need to take some Tylenol if I was going to be able to move.

The only bottle in the house was downstairs in the kitchen, and if I was going to get any relief from the pain, my daughter would have to get the bottle for me. I knew my daughter hated to go downstairs by herself in the early morning when the house was still dark. But with some coaxing, she summoned the courage to go downstairs and get it for me.

Except there wasn't any. As she frantically dug around in the cupboard, as I had described for her, she discovered an empty bottle of Tylenol. I was stuck. I could not move without excruciating pain. How on earth was I going to solve this problem?

I knew my friend from next door wasn't home, so she couldn't come in my house with her key and help me out. And it was early in the morning—too early for my daughter to go to another neighbor and get help. Calling 911 seemed drastic for a back spasm.

Eventually, over an hour later, the pain started to lessen slightly. And with careful movement, I was finally able to get to a standing position. After I had walked around carefully for a while, the pain subsided to the point that I was able to move without intense pain.

The first thing I did was to go to the pharmacy and get a large bottle of pain reliever. Then I made a detailed checklist of all other kinds of remedies I might need in case of emergency. After that, I made sure to check my supply on a regular basis. As a single parent, I couldn't risk being without what I needed ever again.

* * * * * * * *

Getting organized and having a plan in place to manage and be proactive about our family's health needs feels good. When we do these things, we know we are doing the best we can to support our family's health.

This is more than just taking your kids to the doctor when they are sick, although that's a necessary part of acting responsibly as a parent. I'm talking about consistently scheduling everybody's well-care appointments and dental and vision checkups. This also means making sure vaccinations are up-to-date, knowing where to go in an emergency, and having the right things on hand at home to manage minor accidents and illnesses. If we don't stay on top of all health-related things, a health problem could be overlooked. We certainly don't want that to happen.

Here are some ways to manage your family's health:

- Regardless of who pays for your kids' health insurance coverage (you or your former spouse), be sure you have the insurance information you need to make sure your kids get good quality health care in all situations—preventative care, sick care, and emergency care. If a wallet card is not provided by the insurance carrier, take note of the information and carry it with you. Or make a laminated card yourself—whatever it takes to have the information handy.

- Be sure you understand what coverage is provided by your health insurance carrier. What kind of a plan do you have? Is there a deductible that needs to be met before coverage kicks in? Can you go directly to any doctor, including specialists, or is there a referral process from a primary care physician that is needed?

- Do your kids have any special medical needs or allergies? Are there any special supplies or medications you need to have on hand?

- For regular appointments, annual medical check-ups, and dental and vision check-ups, consider scheduling appointments for your kids during their birth month, or during the summer when they are out of school, so it happens at the same time every year. That way, you won't forget. And if possible, schedule their appointments all in one day, so you only have to take time off work once.

- If your child has a medical condition that requires ongoing care, or if she takes daily medication, you'll likely be required to have forms completed by her doctor before she participates in sports, summer camp programs, and the like. Understand what the process is. Where do you get the forms? How long does it take for them to be completed by your doctor? Are signatures required by both parents? Knowing these things in advance will save you time and the stress of getting these forms completed at the last minute.

- At the beginning of cold and flu season each year, stock up on essentials so you are prepared when you need them. Keep a supply of things like children's pain reliever, an easy-read thermometer, cold and cough syrup, cough lozenges, or whatever remedy (drug store or home remedy) you feel is helpful to your kids while they are sick. As a single parent, it is no fun to go to the drug store or pharmacy in the middle of the night. It is even worse if you have to pack up your sick kids and take them with you. Be prepared. Stock up and save yourself the trouble of the potential midnight trip. You'll be glad you did!

Keep on top of your family's health needs. It is an important task, and one that as a parent we can't overlook or put on the back burner. We want our families to be healthy, and being proactive about their health care will help ensure they are.

> **ACTION ITEM:**
> Create a simple emergency sheet for your home. Where is the closest hospital or urgent care center located? How do you get there? Can you go directly there in case of emergency or is some pre-approval required from your insurance company? Take the time to figure out this critical information so you are prepared in case an emergency takes place.

We've learned a *lot* of organizational things in this section—from how to plan your calendar to buying medicine for cold season, and a lot of things in between.

Now that you know how to get your life in order, you can enjoy the benefits of living an organized, and therefore much easier, life. You will be able to keep your family's activities straight by using your new calendaring system, set up a home that feels great and works well for your new life, be in control of your finances and paperwork, provide healthy meals for your family, and take care of everybody's health.

But there are more great things coming! Now that you have some ideas on how to stabilize and organize your life, you are ready to take your life to a whole new level of peace and fulfillment—one where you can live out the things you've already learned.

In the next section, *Get Going—Live it Every Day,* I'll show you how to keep moving forward, and to continue to grow and use the things you've learned in the first two sections. I'll give suggestions on how to manage your energy, understand your changing friendships, and make your kids' homecomings special. Following these tips will inspire you to relax into your stable and organized new life.

3

Get Going—Live it Every Day

CHAPTER 24

Ongoing Growth

Greatness is nothing but many small littles.
— OVID, Roman Poet

* * * * * * * *

One weekend a few years after my divorce, when my daughter was with her dad, I sat alone in the living room of my condo, looking around. It had been a typical weekend for me without her. I'd gotten the necessary errands done, and I was looking forward to her coming back home again.

And then it hit me. Everything was okay. I was doing just fine.

I'd gotten us happily settled into a comfortable, safe, and secure place to live. My life felt organized and solid. My daughter was adjusting well to her schedule of living in two homes. I felt like I had relaxed into my new life and had friends around me for support and fun.

The long, dark post-divorce street that had once stretched out in front of me didn't feel so dark anymore. In fact, there were lots of lights on that street now, and fewer areas were dim. I was making some significant progress.

I'd discovered along the way that there are so many wonderful things life has to offer, but when the view of that is unclear—like it often is when we are in the midst of emotional upheaval—it feels impossible to reach for them.

Now it was time to just…grow; to keep nurturing those things in myself that I'd learned along the way. Practice a little every day. And keep moving forward to where I wanted to go—toward the kind of life I wanted for myself and my daughter.

* * * * * * * *

Personal, ongoing growth is something that just happens, magically, when we nurture and care for ourselves and take the time to learn from what we've experienced. In the previous two sections, we've learned how to stabilize ourselves following our divorce and how to organize our lives so they work and are easy for us to manage as a single parent.

In this section, *Get Going—Live it Every Day,* we're going to take all that knowledge and use it to continue moving forward with our lives. I'll describe the things you can do to keep growing and moving ahead to the life you want—things that will benefit you and your kids. You'll learn how to pace yourself for maximum energy, appreciate what you've achieved, and welcome your kids home after they've been away.

The benefit of doing the things in this section is you will move away from old ways of doing things and from behavior and beliefs that don't serve you anymore. At the same time, you'll move toward the happy life that is waiting for you and your kids.

Not taking this knowledge to heart means we might stay right where we are: and that might be *stuck*. And I don't want anyone to be stuck in their old life. I want us all to be moving toward the life we want.

By the end of this section, you'll have what you need to go confidently toward the new life that you want—

a stabilized, organized, and growth-filled happy life for you and your kids.

ACTION ITEM:

The simple act of reading this book means that you are already growing and moving forward with your life. What progress have you already made? What difference do you see in yourself compared to the way you felt when you first opened this book? Make a list of the three things you see that are already different.

CHAPTER 25

Manage Your Energy

The secret of change is to focus all of your energy, not on fighting the old, but on building the new.
— SOCRATES

* * * * * * * *

I love the day before I leave for vacation. Not just because I'm looking forward to getting away, but because of how much I manage to get done that day. Usually, I have a ton of things to finish before I go — an almost *impossible* number of things — but I somehow manage to complete them all. It feels so good to be that focused.

People always try to figure out how to manage their time. What we need to do is manage our energy. When we do this, we make efficient use of our time by doing things when we feel the most productive. And as a single parent with a lot of things to do, maximizing our efficiency is usually important, especially when our kids are with us.

Managing our energy is the first step toward our ongoing growth in this *Get Going—Live it Every Day* section. It allows us to plan for our day and get things done when our minds and bodies are at their best. And while peak productivity is not always the primary goal, it's certainly nice to use the energy we have to do the things we most want to do, when we want to do them.

The downside of not managing energy can be wasted time and not accomplishing the things we need to get done.

When I have a seemingly impossible number of things to do, and I'm not leaving for vacation the next day, I try to conjure up that same sense of focus. It almost always works, as long as I have a good strategy for my day and I manage my energy more than my time.

Here's what works for me:

Make a list of the absolute must-do items. Rather than starting your day without a plan in place, take a few minutes in the morning—or better yet, the night before—to list what you will accomplish.

Know my most energetic and efficient times of day to get things done. Most people have a pretty good sense of when they are the most productive. Are you a morning person or a night owl? Whatever the case, use that to the fullest advantage and plan your day around that. Knock out the most intense things when your mind is the sharpest or when you're well-rested. And then fit in the other tasks to match your energy level.

Turbo-time and snail-time. We all have 168 hours in every week to spend however we want. If you have a lot of things to do, how can you squeeze the most benefit out of every one of those hours?

Have you ever noticed how, when you are really absorbed in something you enjoy doing, like reading a great book, time seems to pass quickly? And other times, when you are working on something you don't enjoy, or standing in line waiting for something, that time seems to stand still?

Try thinking of time as something that's variable — it shrinks and expands to accommodate the things in our lives as we need it to. I call it turbo-time and snail-time. Do you need to get a huge number of things done, like the night before you leave on a trip? Use turbo-time. Do you want to relax and enjoy a Sunday afternoon? Slow down and adjust yourself to snail-time. Just tap into whichever one you need.

Work smarter. As wonderful as I know you are, you can't be great at doing everything. Do the things you excel at and were meant to do — the things that match up with your skills and special talents, and then hire the rest out or swap services with somebody to do it for you.

Keep yourself in top form. What is your personal formula for having the most energy and getting the most done? For me, that means sleep (a solid eight hours each night), eating healthy food, getting some exercise every day, spending quality time with the people I love, and ten to fifteen minutes of quiet, focused time to prepare for my day.

Now that you've learned these great energy management strategies, you'll feel so efficient you'll be ready to tackle anything that comes your way. Part of managing your energy is knowing when to relax and take time to recharge yourself. In the next chapter, "Relax When Your Kids Are Away," I give you things to consider as you plan your relaxation time.

ACTION ITEM:

When are you the most energetic? When do you need to rest and relax to recharge? Define your current energy cycle.

Are you the kind of person who needs to run five miles every morning just so you can concentrate during the day? Or is an uninterrupted hour of downtime every night so you can watch TV or read a book the thing that keeps you going? Or maybe it's some quiet time in the morning with a cup of coffee? Find whatever it is and use it for maximum energy.

CHAPTER 26

Relax When Your Kids Are Away

*I'm having fruit salad for dinner. Well, it's
mostly grapes actually. Ok, all grapes. Fermented
grapes. I'm having wine for dinner.*
— UNKNOWN

• • • • • • • •

As a single parent, you probably don't have very many chances to relax when your kids are around. So the time to recharge yourself is when they aren't with you, so you are rested and refreshed and have maximum energy for them when they are with you again. If you don't take time to relax when your kids are away, you run the risk of becoming depleted—a state where you will lack the energy and patience to deal with them when they come back.

When I became a single parent, I found that I had a lot of free time on weekends that I didn't have before. So I came up with a list of things that I could do to relax on my own time. Since I love to do home improvement and decorating projects, I spent a lot of time going through open houses when homes were for sale in my neighborhood to get decorating ideas. And I made elaborately time-consuming trips to places like *The Container Store,* where I could lose myself in the rows of baskets and organizational supplies that fascinate me.

Here are a few things to consider when planning your relaxation time:

Plan activities that are "tank-filling" for you. What do you enjoy doing when you have free, unstructured time? What things bring you joy, and leave you inspired or motivated? You have an endless list of possible things you can do when your kids aren't with you. Choose a few that make you feel good and plan to do them this week or the next time your kids are away. Doing this will fill your emotional tank and allow you to have a break, so you have more energy for them when they return to you.

Have that extra glass of wine *after* the kids leave. If drinking alcohol is something that's relaxing to you, be careful about doing it when the kids are in your care, or any time close to when they *will* be in your care. Better yet, if you do drink, drink on your own time, in the company and safety of your own friends, when there is *no* possibility of your former spouse ever getting the impression that you've had too much to drink.

This is especially important if drinking or alcohol-related problems played any part in the breakdown of your marriage. Any sign of intoxication — even just once — could cause your former spouse to wonder if it's something that happens regularly, and if the safety of your kids is ever in question.

Save dating for when your kids are not with you. You probably don't have your children twenty-four hours a day, seven days a week, so if you are going to date or spend romantic time with another adult, do it when your kids aren't with you. Make that choice for their sake. Keep that part of your life separate until you are at the point in a relationship where you know it's serious, and you plan to be together permanently. Your kids have been through a lot of adjustments recently, and if you introduce somebody new to them too soon, they will be confused about where to attach emotionally.

Find a way to take a break if your kids are with you all the time. This book was written mainly for women who are raising kids that live in two homes, which means that your kids are only with you part of the time. For those of you who do have your kids all the time, it's important that you find a way to get regular breaks, and have time to rest and recharge without them, so you are refreshed when you do have them.

Do whatever it takes to set this up. If you have family members or friends who can help you, ask them. If you don't, find a way to trade childcare days with another single friend, even if it only happens a few times a year. Every once in a while is better than not at all. But please, for your sake and sanity, find a way.

If you are someone who is used to managing things on your own, asking for help so you can get some rest may feel a little weird at first. The next chapter covers why, as single parents, it's important to ask for help.

ACTION ITEM:

What's the most relaxing thing you can provide for yourself besides sleeping? Can you schedule it into your life the next time your kids are away?

CHAPTER 27

Ask For Help

Sometimes the only answer people are looking for when they ask for help is that they won't have to face the problem alone.
— MARK AMEND

* * * * * * * *

One morning I couldn't leave home because my car wouldn't start. It was on a holiday, and while I wasn't headed to work that morning, I was planning to do a bunch of shopping-related errands—things that I felt needed to get done.

The auto-repair shop was closed because of the holiday, so I knew I had to get a rental car that day if I was going to get my errands done.

I felt like I just couldn't ask my friends for help. They'd already made plans for a fun day, and I didn't want to inconvenience anybody with helping me pick up a rental car. I felt like I'd been leaning pretty heavily on everyone during the previous few months as I went through the changes related to my divorce. This request on top of all of that seemed like too much.

So I decided to walk to the rental car agency, which was only about a mile from my house. Then I remembered it was closed, due to the holiday. The next closest location that was open was at the airport, half an hour away by car.

Then the situation snowballed; one bad decision turned into two until things just got ridiculous.

I called a cab to take me to the airport rental car location. There weren't very many cars available—again, because of that darn holiday—so I ended up paying way more for the car than would have normally been the case. Then I chose the *return to different location* option that added even more to the cost of the rental car. By the time I was on my way, the cost of solving the problem of my car not running was not worth what I was gaining by doing my needed errands that day.

Looking back now, I can see that I was so hell-bent on solving the problem myself, and not appearing needy by asking for help, that I lost all sense of perspective on the issue. It was a crazy way to handle the problem, but at the time I thought I was doing the right thing.

And the worst part? When I told my friend later about what had happened, she said, "Oh, you should have just asked me. Our extra car just sat on the street all day. We weren't using it." Groan.

＊ ＊ ＊ ＊ ＊ ＊ ＊ ＊

We don't have to do everything by ourselves. Asking for help with things that we don't know how to do (like setting up a new computer system), or we can't do (like stay home from work every time our kids are sick), or we can't possibly manage alone (like moving furniture) is the right thing to do, because it is impossible to handle everything on our own.

When we ask people for help, we develop and strengthen our relationships with those who help us. Many of us hesitate to ask for help because we worry about being intrusive or needy, when in reality, most people love to help, and it is very satisfying to them.

So when you need it, ask for help! Whether it's from a sister, friend, parent, or employer, it doesn't matter. Just ask.

Asking for help is an area of my own life where I do a pretty lousy job. I grew up with a belief that I could figure things out myself — that I could fix things, handle things, move things, and build things without asking for much, if any, help. And I never wanted to be *that* person, that needy person who was always asking for help in some way, that person who couldn't figure things out for herself. Ugh, how unappealing, I thought.

What I didn't know was how important it is to get the support of other people who are ready and willing to give it; to be honest with people and tell them, "I'm feeling scared, or overwhelmed, or I'm struggling, and I need some help. Can you help me?"

When we ask people for help, we build two-way connections with them. The helper feels great for helping. And the person being helped gets the relief they need.

I know I *love* to help people. I love it when they ask me, because I like to feel useful and that I've made a difference to somebody's day. All someone needs to say is, "Can you help me with (fill in the blank)?" and I'm on the task. I expect the same is true for many people.

So rather than waiting until you are in a dire circumstance, instead, consider who you could ask for help. It can't hurt. They may not be able to help you, and that's okay. But the next person will likely be able to.

Before you struggle — simply ask.

As for me? I'm still learning the new behavior of asking for help. I try to remember that I can't do everything all the time. And that it's okay to ask.

Sometimes the best way to adopt a new behavior is to think about somebody who you admire and respect, and imagine behaving the same way they do. In the next chapter, "Find Mentors," I'll show you what a big difference a good mentor can make in your life.

> **ACTION ITEM:**
>
> Right now, with your life and all the things going on in it, where do you need help the most? Who could you ask to help you with this? Now call or email them and ask them to help you.

CHAPTER 28

Find Mentors

*If you cannot see where you are going, ask
someone who has been there before.*
— J. LOREN NORRIS

* * * * * * * *

When I was in my mid-twenties, I had the great fortune of
working with an amazing woman named Audrey. Almost twenty
years older than me, Audrey was a lot farther along in her career
in operations management than I was. Up until that point in my
professional life, I had spent almost all of my time working with
men. So meeting Audrey—a woman with a sky-high degree of
integrity, confidence, and a direct approach to solving problems—was something that made a big impact on me.

Audrey had the knack of everything. Because of her com-
mon-sense attitude, she could diagnose and fix problems quite
easily. She didn't concern herself with office politics; she pretty
much just called things as she saw them. Her straightforward
style didn't mesh well with everybody, but it certainly allowed her
to get a lot accomplished. And for a young woman like me, just
starting out in the business world, she was an excellent mentor.

Years later, whenever I found myself in a business situation
where I wasn't sure what to do or the best way to solve a
problem, I would ask myself, "What would Audrey do?" Then

I would try to remember how it felt to work with her, what she would likely say, and how she'd handle the situation. And the answer would come.

* * * * * * * *

Sometimes we need a little nudge to get unstuck from something. When options seem limited or unclear and we aren't sure what to do, having mentors—or people who we respect and whose behavior we can imitate—can give us the boost to keep moving.

We can ask ourselves, "What would my mentor do in this situation?" just like I did in the story about Audrey. This works well, and usually leads to the answer we need.

Not having a mentor isn't going to make your life worse, but you'll find that *having* one will make it a lot better.

I've always had a huge interest in the world of self-help and positive psychology. During my divorce, I dug in by reading anything I could get my hands on related to healing my life and moving forward. I developed a pool of mentors in the form of writers and people whose experiences I could relate to and was motivated and encouraged by. It was like they became my trusted friends during a tough time.

For areas where I needed help, I also learned to listen to friends and colleagues for ideas and clues from their experiences. They were my informal mentors, and I tried to find the one thing I could learn from each of them. My friend Tami taught me things about cooking that I'd never considered, Janelle taught me how to *really* get organized, and Kathleen was a wonderful role model for somebody rebuilding her life.

When someone does something well, figure out what made her succeed and then incorporate those same traits into your life.

Getting unstuck by imitating the behavior of a mentor will get us moving forward again. And before we know it, we'll be achieving things and getting stuff crossed off our lists—which is great, since there are plenty of things to get done as a single parent! In the next chapter, I'll show you how to make a "done-it" list, which will allow you to take stock of all the things you do get done.

ACTION ITEM:

Is there a person in your life who you admire and whose views on life you respect? Ask him or her to be your mentor!

Another option is to create an imaginary mentor committee. Add your perfect mentor candidates to it and copy the parts of their lives and behaviors that you admire. Who are they? Your mom? Your boss? Oprah? Your best friend? Then, when you get in situations you can't figure out, call on your imaginary mentors to advise you.

CHAPTER 29

Make a Done-it List

Nothing builds self-esteem and self-confidence like accomplishment.
— THOMAS CARLYLE

* * * * * * * *

There are experts all over the place who tell us everything from how to take care of our health to how to do our taxes. All of these things require making a list of some sort, beginning something, and focusing on what you haven't done yet.

How about reversing that? Make a "done-it" list to track all the things you *have* accomplished in any given day, week, month, or year. When you do this, you'll be surprised, motivated and inspired by all you've done. You'll also get a huge sense of accomplishment and feel good about yourself.

I tried this at the end of 2014. I went through my calendar and personal records and listed all the things I had done so that I could get an idea of the volume of things I had accomplished during the year. I listed the events I attended, the trips I took, the healthcare appointments I'd made (and kept!), the parties I went to, and more.

It was astounding! The sheer volume of things I had done was so motivating that it made me really excited about the upcoming year and all the things I planned to accomplish.

Plus, it helped to get some perspective on not just the big event-type things I had done, but also all the little things I do every day, week, and year that keep my life running smoothly.

I suspect the same will be true for you. It's easy to focus on what *isn't* getting done and to feel overwhelmed by what is in front of you. But if you take a moment to reflect on all you *have* done, rather than the lack, I think you'll be surprised by how much there is on your list.

Here's a glimpse of what your done-it list for just one week might include:

- Woke kids up, fed them and got them to school: 5 times
- Worked at my job: 5 days
- Picked kids up after school, drove to lessons: 3 times
- Made dinner: 5 times
- Made lunches for school: 5 times
- Helped kids with homework: 5 times
- Bath time, reading, put kids to bed: 5 times
- Loads of laundry: 6
- Grocery store: 2 trips
- Went to yoga class
- Shopped for soccer shoes for daughter
- Filled car with gas
- Made dentist appointment
- Paid bills online
- Completed forms for the upcoming class trip
- Attended parent-teacher conference at son's school
- Went out to dinner with friends
- Watched a movie

All the things that will appear on your done-it list are a sign of not only the things you have accomplished, but also the progress you are making in building a new life for yourself.

Great work! You are adapting to and embracing this new life of yours. That's real, personal, ongoing growth, which means another step down that street toward your new life.

Sometimes the kind of personal growth we are experiencing causes changes in our friendships. In the next chapter, I show you the different things that can happen to our friendships during this period of our lives.

ACTION ITEM:

Take a look through your calendar and get an idea of all the things you did in the last week. I bet you'll be amazed at all the things you accomplished! You can even sign up for a cool app called *iDoneThis* to help you out with this at idonethis.com.

CHAPTER 30

Understand that Friendships May Change

*Surround yourself with only people who
are going to lift you higher.*
— OPRAH WINFREY

• • • • • • • •

It was during dinner with two friends from work that Jessica decided she had to find her own way to navigate her divorce process. Going the typical way that society and those well-meaning friends advised just wasn't working. "Find a tough lawyer!" "Stand your ground!" Everybody had advice for her. It was kind of like the unsolicited advice she got when she was a new mom. People seemed to come out of the woodwork to tell her what they thought she should or shouldn't do.

Despite suggestions from these friends and her lawyer, Jessica just didn't feel that taking an adversarial position in her divorce would give her the end result she was looking for, or one that she could feel any sense of closure about. That just wasn't her; she wasn't a fighter. And as angry as she was with her former husband, she knew this wasn't the way to proceed.

So Jessica told her friends she was taking a different path with her divorce—one that didn't include lawyers and fighting. Still, they couldn't drop it. They disagreed so strongly with her decision that it affected their friendship with her. Instead of being supportive, their agenda for how Jessica should handle the situation took over.

It was too bad because this disagreement caused the loss of their friendships — ones that Jessica didn't ever imagine she would lose. She accepted it though, as a part of her whole divorce process, and tried to let them go with grace. Soon, new friends who were able to support her decision for how to handle her divorce came into her life.

* * * * * * * *

When couples divorce, it affects so many more people than just the couple or family involved.

Sometimes friends become conflicted about what to do or say and who to support, which means that friendships that have been in place for years sometimes change. Sometimes friends even disagree with the reason the divorce is happening in the first place, and when they express how they feel, hurt feelings result.

It's important to understand and recognize that this may happen, so you aren't taken by surprise if it does. Otherwise, you may not understand why some of the friendships you have — maybe even long-time friendships — start to change.

Extended families are impacted, too. Sometimes these family members withdraw in an attempt to stay neutral. And if there was a significant or public event that caused the marriage to end, that makes it even tougher. For the person in the middle of the divorce, this can be difficult and confusing to sort out.

I found that friendships change like this:

You lose some. In an effort to be supportive, friends sometimes take sides. Less commonly, friendships stay in place with both parties. But usually, friends feel some need to form an allegiance with one side or the other, and, as a result, friendships can fade away. It may feel hurtful when this happens, but it is natural reaction and something to be expected.

You gain some. New schedules and life changes have a way of causing new people to appear. I met new friends because I was in different places, at different times than when I had been married. And I met some people who were experiencing the same thing as me. I also started a new job during my divorce process and gained some wonderful new friends through that experience.

You keep some. Your close friends will stick with you. You know who they are. Be careful with these friends, though. Be cautious of their anger on your behalf. Sometimes in their attempt to care about you and support you, they push you into an adversarial position with your former spouse that doesn't serve you well.

Shift happens. You never know when a former acquaintance will shift into a friend. Just like in the "gain some" category, life's circumstances can cause changes in friendships — people you've known casually now become close friends. Maybe it's the single woman down the street, who you've always wanted to start a friendship with, and now you have the time to do that. Perhaps it's the guy at work, who shares the same love of music as you. Be on the lookout for these opportunities to bring new friends into your life.

Yes, your friendships will likely change. If you lose a few, let them go with grace; release them with understanding as part of your transition to a new life. You may also gain some wonderful new friends. Be open to all the changes that may happen.

Part of ongoing growth is letting go of the limiting belief that there is only one way to do things. Another important aspect of being open to change is how we view special dates and events in our lives. In the next chapter, I describe how you can release yourself from the power that a calendar date can have on you.

ACTION ITEM:

Are you holding tightly to a friendship that would be better to release at this point?

Don't pursue this person or try to contact them this week. If they call, decline the request to do something together until you are clear about how you feel.

CHAPTER 31

Release Yourself from the Power of a (Calendar) Date

The best things in life are the people you love, the places you've seen, and the memories you've made along the way.
— UNKNOWN

* * * * * * * *

One day while I was watching *Oprah* on TV, Nate Berkus, an interior designer, TV personality, and one of Oprah's inside guys, was there as her guest. He told her the story of how he had lost his partner in the tragic 2004 Indian Ocean tsunami. They were on holiday in Sri Lanka when the disaster struck. Nate survived, but sadly, his partner Fernando did not.

The experience was terrible for Nate—so horrific it would be unimaginable to many. But there was Nate, a few years later, functioning again. He happened to be on Oprah's show on the same day as a woman who had lost her child and was suffering unspeakable grief. Nate had some great advice for her, which was to not give power to dates or anniversaries.

Nate suggested that, following a loss, a lot of people can't deal with special dates or anniversaries, and that this is expected and understandable. It is normal to be sad. But it is also possible that eventually, you might wake up on that date and be okay. He advised that we let our feelings come when they want to come, and then we won't have to live in fear of those anniversary dates. In essence, don't give them any power.

I took Nate's advice to heart that day, and it is something I have initiated since then. I believe this applies to holidays and special days, and how we handle them as single parents.

* * * * * * * *

As single parents, our custody schedule and calendar typically lays out which days of the year our kids will be with us. And usually, that calendar specifies when our kids are with us on special dates and holidays. If you take a less rigid approach to how you view those special dates, by being flexible about when they are celebrated and not worrying about whether or not it is on the exact day, it will be far less stressful for you.

Holidays, birthdays, and other special days only come once a year. And the likelihood is, you will need to share them with your former spouse.

But there can be huge flexibility in when special dates are celebrated or observed. Looking back years later, your kids won't remember that they celebrated a holiday on a different date; they will remember the fun times you had together. On the other hand, if what they remember is being shuttled back and forth between homes and trying to always squeeze two holidays out of one day, and the pressure associated with that, those memories will lock in forever.

In my family, Christmas has been celebrated as early as December 21st or as late as December 30th. It's much more important to us that we are all together than it is to celebrate on the exact day. Plus, celebrating Christmas on the day that works for our family allows for the possibility that Christmas Eve and Christmas Day are open and available for my daughter to enjoy in her other home—and relieves a lot of pressure in trying to make arrangements that suit everybody.

Make it easy for yourself and everybody else. Build in some flexibility to how you view holidays and special dates and release yourself from the power of the actual date itself. You will be glad to see your kids whenever that happens, no matter when it is. Make it work for you.

Now that you've learned a helpful way to view how special dates are celebrated and observed, you are ready to learn how to make the homecoming experience for your kids go smoothly and peacefully every time.

ACTION ITEM:

Do you have a date, holiday, or event that feels sacred to you? How could you reinvent it so that the exact date doesn't matter?

CHAPTER 32

Make Their Homecoming Special

What I love most about my home is who I share it with.
— TAD CARPENTER

* * * * * * * *

My friend Sandi used to tackle home improvement and other general projects when her kids were away with their dad for the weekend. Then, when they arrived back home to her place, she made a game out of them finding what was new in the house. Sometimes it was a small thing, like hanging a new picture on the wall; other times it was a bigger thing, like a new piece of furniture or a painted bookcase.

She would also take careful note of what her kids asked for, and try to make, clean, or fix it when they were gone. She did things like hot-gluing the patches her son had earned onto his sports bag, spray-painting the recycled light fixture her daughter wanted for her bedroom and making double batches of their favorite snack mix. Then when they came home, they'd look around to find what had changed since they'd been gone.

It was a simple tradition, but it was the perfect thing to help her kids transition back to her home after they'd been gone.

* * * * * * * *

It feels so good to know that somebody's glad to see you. Our kids feel that same way. Even though their schedule may require that they divide their time between your home and their dad's place, and the going back and forth thing becomes a regular pattern, they want to feel welcomed and loved every time they come back to your place.

When you do that for them, they get that ongoing sense of belonging that only coming home can bring. And we want them to feel that, right? Because transitions back and forth between homes can be hard on kids, even if both places are familiar to them.

How about making it a habit to make their homecoming special? Whether this is monthly, weekly or a few times a week doesn't matter. What can you do so they know you are glad to see them—every single time they return home to your place?

Here are a few things that have worked for me:

I bake cookies, muffins, or something equally yummy, so it smells good when my daughter comes in the house. If your kids prefer to help with the baking, have everything ready when they come home. This works regardless of your kids' ages!

Watch a favorite television show or movie together. We have a few shows we like to watch and that we only watch if we're together. Depending on the time of day she returns, sometimes we watch a long-anticipated show or movie together. We even made a pact to not watch the show while we are apart, so that one of us is not ahead of the other.

Take a walk together, walk the dog, or go for a bike ride. Physical activity can create a great transition. Run around and get everybody all tired out. Then, come home and relax together.

Do a craft or play a game. Choose something you enjoy doing together. It can be anything, and will vary depending on the age of your kids. This could be drawing, cooking, playing board games, or listening to music; it doesn't matter what it is, as long as it's something everybody likes doing. If you have a few kids and there isn't agreement on a favorite, switch back and forth on which activity you'll do when they return. This doesn't have to take up a lot of time. Even 30 minutes or so will help everybody settle back into a feeling of familiarity.

Do whatever makes the transition back easier. Take the time to talk about what's been happening the last few days. Plan what will happen in the coming days or weeks until the next transition point. Some of the best conversations with our kids happen when there is another activity going on. Keep them involved, talking, and playing, or whatever it takes so they can relax and feel at home again.

What our kids want is for us to be sincerely interested in and engaged with them, regardless of their age. In the next chapter, "Have Faith in What You Offer Your Kids," I describe how to use your strengths and specialties so that these have a big impact on your time together.

ACTION ITEM:

What activity can you plan so your kids will transition to your home more easily? What tradition can you start doing so the feeling they get when they come home to your place is the same every time? Whatever you settle on, plan to start doing it this week.

CHAPTER 33

Have Faith in What You Offer Your Kids

Our deepest fear is not that we are inadequate. Our deepest fear is that we are powerful beyond measure.
— MARIANNE WILLIAMSON

. . . .

I have a friend who has this ongoing problem. His former wife makes oodles of money and positions herself as the classic *Disneyland* parent by constantly buying things for their kids. There is no way he can compete with that. Nor should he try. To do that would contradict the things he values, and would change the kind of things he models for his kids. More importantly, the kids would lose out on all the great things he has to offer that aren't related to money or stuff.

He's a great dad. He spends as much quality time as possible with his kids. He's set up his life in such a way that he's fully focused on the kids when he's with them, and gives them the love and attention that they not only want, but will remember. He reads stories to them every night. They go for long bike rides, explore their local parks, and make elaborate baking messes in the kitchen. And the kids love it. They can't wait for dad time.

. . . .

Just like in junior high, when there was always somebody who seemed smarter, more popular, or who had better stuff, you might feel a sense of competition with your child's other home. Often, those feelings take place because you are comparing what you can buy for your kids or how much time you spend with them, to what happens with their other parent.

Have faith in what you offer your kids. They love you for being you, not for trying to be like somebody else. The things that make you special and that you enjoy doing with your kids are yours alone; they won't get that from their other parent. And regardless of whether or not you can give them all the things you want to, when you spend quality time with them doing something together that you enjoy, they will love it.

Kids are smart. They know the difference between a parent who is sincerely engaged with them and one who is going through the motions.

You may not have all the resources you want—financial or time—to give endlessly to your kids, and that's okay. Make good use of what you do have. Make it count. Instead of buying things, whenever you can, *do* things together that create those wonderful, forever-lasting childhood memories.

In my home, the thing I focus most on offering my daughter is my time. When she was younger, I arranged my business hours so I could be home in the afternoon when she got home from school. As she's gotten older and become involved in after-school activities, I make sure we have time in the evenings to just talk.

Sometimes it's on the couch in the family room, when she's taking a break from homework. Or sometimes it's when we're doing the dishes, driving in the car, or—most precious to me of all—sitting on her bed at night before she goes to sleep. We talk about friends, school troubles, art projects, YouTube Vloggers, and anything else on her mind. This is a sacred time, because I know how important it is in the grand scheme of what I offer to her as her mom.

Understanding the importance of what we can provide and do for our kids is an important step in growing into our new lives. It helps us become more aware of our strengths and appreciate our areas of excellence. When we learn to do that, it's a lot easier for us to take the long view on how to get along with our former spouse. In the next chapter, I show you why it's important to do that.

> **ACTION ITEM:**
>
> What is one great thing you can do this week with your kids that is within your means, and more importantly, takes advantage of your strengths, superpowers, and enthusiasm? Do that.

CHAPTER 34

If You See a Chance, Take It

Life goes on…whether you choose to move on and
take a chance in the unknown. Or stay behind, locked
in the past, thinking of what could have been.
— STEPHANIE SMITH

* * * * * * * *

Meredith's parents divorced when she was about five years
old. From that time until she was sixteen, she split her time
between both parents' homes, living half-time with each. This
was an exhausting, frustrating experience for her for almost the
entire time. Her parents didn't agree on much, the rules were
different in both homes, and it felt like a constant battle. Dana,
her mom, and Julie, her stepmom, didn't see eye-to-eye on
anything, and pretty much went out of their way to make life
difficult for each other. It was a tough way to grow up.

But time changes things.

Today, Dana and Julie are not just friendly toward each other,
they are actually friends. They both show up (together!) at
events to support Meredith, they meet for dinner, and they've
even gone away for girls' weekends together.

So what happened? How did things change?

Meredith says it was a slow process. It didn't happen overnight, and it wasn't connected to any one event. Rather, it was

a lot of maturing that occurred slowly over the years. Dana and Julie eventually realized that their constant fighting was really hurting Meredith. They met one day and agreed to start working together, both for Meredith's sake and for each other.

They built a new relationship on that. Once they began to trust each other, it all got a lot easier.

* * * * * * * *

You may be at odds with your former spouse right now, and it might be that way for a long time. But hopefully, there will come a time when you are ready to move past that point.

It doesn't matter whether you just separated or if you have been divorced for years — if you see a chance to improve the way you work with him and treat him, take it!

Improved interaction between the two of you will benefit everybody — especially your kids. You'll be a good example for them by showing what it's like to treat him respectfully. So don't get stuck in the rut of feeling like your relationship needs to be an ongoing battlefield. It's okay, and preferred, to get along.

And remember, you are both on the same team here. You are raising your kids together. You both have their best interest at heart. So take the long view on this, not the short view. There will be an endless number of things you'll be doing together with your kids over the years, like graduations, weddings, grandchildren, and more.

It will be a lot more comfortable for everybody involved if you can get along with each other. So whenever and if ever you see a chance to make peace with him, take it! Whether it is six months from now or 20 years from now, it is *never* too late to get along.

Life is complicated at the best of times. But when you are a single parent rebuilding a life for yourself and your kids, it can get even more difficult. In the next chapter, I describe the value of keeping your life as simple as possible.

ACTION ITEM:

What one thing can you do to move toward a better relationship with your former spouse? You have the advantage of knowing about the important things in his life. Could you send a quick happy birthday email? Or offer to drop off the kids if you know his schedule is tight? Decide on something and do it.

CHAPTER 35

Keep It Simple

*Maintaining a complicated life is a
great way to avoid changing it.*
— ELAINE ST. JAMES

* * * * * * *

When I was getting divorced, and in the years following,
I focused on getting a lot of things done when my daughter
wasn't with me. That's when I did most of the time-consuming
daily business of living things, like grocery shopping, cleaning
the house, paying bills, and paperwork. That way, I had plenty
of time available to focus on her and the things she needed
when she was with me.

This made my alone time busier, but created a lot of simplicity
in the parenting-time part of my life. And in the long run, that
paid off for me. I didn't feel rushed to get things done when
she was with me. Our time together was usually very relaxed,
and we had plenty of time to do things we enjoyed. By doing
a little planning, I was able to keep my life very simple.

* * * * * * *

There's no denying it — this single parenting thing is not
easy. Nothing about it is easy. So whenever and wherever
possible, *make it* easier for yourself. Choose to make your

new life work *for* you, not against you, by keeping your life as simple as possible.

Sometimes choosing simplicity means taking what seems like the harder path first. This can mean doing things like shopping and household chores when you have free time without your kids so that things are easier when they are with you. Those kinds of "get it done now to make it simpler later" things really make a difference in making your life feel simplified.

The law of parsimony (also called Occam's razor) says that, all things being equal between two ideas, the simpler one is preferable and more likely to be correct. Or put another way, when in doubt, choose the simplest option.

Do yourself a big favor and make life easy for yourself wherever possible. Use the ideas I suggest in this book to simplify your life and get things done so you can spend more quality time with your kids. Then, instead of trying to do everything, choose the things that are important to you and focus on those. Save your energy for the things that are important, like being home when your kids are, and being available to talk when they need you.

Even though it may seem like you have a long road ahead of you, it is amazing how quickly the time goes. Your kids are only with you at home for a limited number of years. Depending on their ages when you divorce, you may only have them in your everyday care for a few more years. All too soon, they will be off to college or working, and away from your everyday responsibility.

When in doubt about a decision, after considering the best option for your kids, choose the option that will keep your life the simplest. I think you'll find that choosing simplicity first will ultimately be the best decision for both you and your kids.

The decision to choose simplicity contributes to an overall feeling of success as we continue to grow and flourish in our new lives. This is an important part of creating the life we want for ourselves. And in moving toward that new life, we may need to adjust our view of ourselves to align with the reality of what's happening. Sometimes we need to reframe things to see them accurately.

In the next chapter, "Figure Out What Success Means to You," I ask how you see yourself, and how you can define your personal sense of success.

ACTION ITEM:
What is one area of your life that is unnecessarily complicated? What one thing could you do to simplify it?

CHAPTER 36

Figure Out What Success Means to You

Be who you are and say what you feel because those who mind don't matter and those who matter don't mind.
— DR. SEUSS

* * * * * * * *

How I defined my own success during my divorce depended a lot on where I was in the process.

Initially, it was basic decisions like understanding the divorce steps that were underway and creating a new routine for my daughter and I that allowed me to move forward from one day to the next. Essentially, it meant taking one more step down that street that felt dark and unfamiliar.

Then it was educating myself on how to do things I hadn't previously been responsible for or managed while I was married, like doing the maintenance work on my home. And later, it was feeling organized because I'd completely revamped the way I managed my finances, so I could keep my home-life and business-life running smoothly. Eventually, it was buying a home on my own, creating new traditions for myself and my daughter, and fully accepting my new life.

* * * * * * * *

The definition of success is different for each of us. It's different because we all have different lives, different stories, different capabilities, and different goals. When we figure out what success means to us, we can gauge ourselves and our progress by that definition. On the other hand, if we compare ourselves to others and to what success means to them, we'll be trying to achieve somebody else's version of success, not ours. And that won't feel very good.

As we go through our divorce, we often feel anything *but* successful. We are usually adapting to all kinds of changes. Some will feel good and empowering. Others, not at all. It may seem like people have all kinds of advice about what we should do, how we should feel, and what we should have already done.

This may cause us to feel like we have failed. But go easy here. This is a situation where no opinion other than yours matters. You are the only person who knows the reality of both your old life and what it is changing to. And only *you* get to determine how you feel and what success is to you.

So what is that for you?

It may be freedom from an oppressive situation or relationship. It may be a decision to take a leap of faith and go back to school or to learn a new skill. It may be interacting with your family in a different way, or the decision to stop destructive behavior.

Success may be finalizing — or beginning — the process of working out your divorce settlement agreement with your former spouse. It may be settling your kids and household into a new home or community, or peacefully transitioning your kids to a schedule where they are comfortable living in two homes. It may be learning to manage your finances or adjusting to being alone on weekends.

You may be looking at your current situation and making choices and decisions for yourself and your family, decisions that allow you to grow and move forward, using the information you have right now, based on what's happening in your life. To me, that forward movement is success. And knowing that you're doing all you can, despite circumstances that may have once seemed overwhelming—that too is success.

There are so many ways to define success at this point in your life. And when we tune in to the things that are working in our lives—the things that are already making us feel successful—it's easier to continue doing them and building on them. When we build on them, we keep growing. And that's something to celebrate. In the last chapter, "Celebrate Your Progress," you'll learn why it's so important to cheer yourself along.

ACTION ITEM:

What is one thing that would feel like success for you right now? What would it take to get there? Are there a couple of "little wins" that would make a big difference to you at this point? What do you have to do to make that happen?

CHAPTER 37

Celebrate Your Progress

*And the day came when the risk it took to remain tight in
the bud became greater than the risk it took to blossom.*

—ANAÏS NIN

• • • • • • •

One day, a few years after my divorce, I went back to the
beach—back to the place where I had felt such deep despair
when my divorce was first happening.

And this time, when the breeze came in the window of the
car, it didn't feel like it would knock me over. Instead, I felt
grounded and stable. I sat there for a long time and thought
about how my life had changed and all that I had learned.
And then, with a simple celebration of the heart, I privately
acknowledged everything that had changed.

I was my own anchor. I was a solid presence for myself, my
daughter, my family, and my friends.

I had figured out how to stabilize myself following my divorce
by caring for my emotional and physical health and giving
myself time to heal.

I had organized my life by effectively managing my finances
and establishing a great place to live.

And I was moving forward. I had embraced my new life, and
my daughter was flourishing.

• • • • • • •

Progress isn't obvious to us when we are looking forward. When the thing we are focused on is in front of us, we are always looking ahead. And that's a good thing.

The only way to see our progress is to turn around and look back.

When we acknowledge the progress we've made and appreciate the effort it took to get to this place, it inspires us to continue on. Failure to do this means we've missed a great chance to cheer ourselves on, and that's just too precious to miss out on.

Stop and look back down that long road and take note of how far you've come. How have you changed? What have you learned? Where are you now compared to where you were when your divorce occurred?

Take the time to notice the new feeling of stability you have now. Observe the organization that you have built into your world. Relish and appreciate the life you now have.

Without looking back, you might not see for yourself how far you've come, how much you've grown, and the progress you've made.

ACTION ITEM:

With an understanding of the progress you've made in your new life, construct a celebration plan for yourself. Your celebration can be whatever you want, but for something deeply personal like this, it may be best viewed as a secret celebration of the heart.

None of the things I describe in this chapter or this book are arbitrary ideas. You can implement them in your life right now, starting today. They will take some effort, and you may need to change how you think about your life in order to do them. But the effort will be well worth it. Collectively, they will make a difference. I promise you that.

I hope you take away from this book the belief that you *are* okay, you *can* do this, and that it's possible to rebuild a happy new life for yourself and your kids — a life that is perfectly suited to you, because you took the time to get stabilized, and then organized, and are now growing and living it every day.

Conclusion

If you want your life to be a magnificent story, then begin by realizing that you are the author and every day you have the opportunity to write a new page.
— MARK HOULAHAN

• • • • • • • •

I'm a firm believer in the idea that we can create the kind of life we want for ourselves; nobody else gets a vote on that. And nobody else can determine how we feel about something, how we structure our new life for our kids, or how we choose to learn new things.

Looking back now, years after my divorce, I see that the things I learned during that time and the things I chose to change have had a long-term influence on me. That old chapter of my life is long past, and now new chapters have emerged.

I've made some colossal screw-ups along the way. I've also had some amazing moments of grace. And when I've learned from the mistakes I've made, and handled things differently, I've made real progress.

My journey to a happy life includes a great new chapter. I was already well on my way to the new life I wanted when I reconnected with my childhood friend, Tom. We were married in 2009. Now I have a wonderful new life—one that is very different than I imagined it would be when I started this journey.

What new chapters are yet to unfold in your life?

I hope as you've read this book you've learned that you are not alone in this. From where I stand, I'm cheering like crazy for you as you write your own new story.

And as you move forward with your new life, I hope you amaze yourself with how stable you are, how organized your life has become, and how you are growing into the future you want.

Acknowledgments

This book would not have been written if it weren't for the inspiration and encouragement of a group of amazing women I had the honor of spending a week with in Paris, in April of 2012. Thank you to Lisa Umberger Arundale, Doni Belau, Kim Davis, Jill Dulitsky, Jamie Eslinger, Angela Ittu, Susan Kruger, Debbie Phillips, Tandi Musuraca Squire, and Michelle Whittaker. You helped me realize there was a book inside me that was worth writing, and that I had the street cred to do it. For this, I am deeply grateful.

To my editing team at Author Bridge Media: Thank you to Kristine Serio, Helen Chang, and Laurie Aranda for your leadership, talent, and hard work. You got me to the finish line.

To the women who shared their stories in this book: Thank you to Cheryl, Vicki, Kim, Shawn, Angie, Ann, Audrey, Mimi, Jessica, Sandi, Dana, Julie, and Meredith. Thank you for your courage. Other women will benefit.

To Nancy Bickford: Thank you for fighting fiercely for those who need your help, and for walking the perfect line between compassion and intensity when I needed it most.

To my cheering section while this book was in progress: Thank you to Denise Dwyer, Janelle Gilbert, Alease Johnson, Tracy Kesselhaut, Neil and Yvonne Ostrander, Tami Ratliffe, Mike Sullivan, Joanne Turnbull, and Alex Velasquez for checking on my progress and encouraging me when I got bogged down. It made a huge difference to me.

To Rob Berkley and Debbie Phillips: Thank you for planting the seed of belief that I had a story to tell, and for the ongoing encouragement to do it. Your influence and support has had an enormous impact.

To my friend, Michelle Piper: Thank you for your wisdom, advice and wholehearted support.

To my father-in-law, Alan Adams: Thank you for the reminder to keep it practical. It kept me focused and on-track.

To my parents, Ross and Nancy Turnbull: Growing up in your home—a place where organization played an important part—I gained the tools and experience to write this book. Thank you for believing in me and for your enthusiasm and encouragement for this project.

To my sisters, Mary Lou Turnbull and Lori Osinga: Thank you for listening to all the iterations and ideas for this book, for giving valuable feedback and never-ending support, and for laughing and crying with me through to the last page.

To my stepsons, Sawyer and Knox Adams: Thank you for making the job of being a stepmom so incredibly easy. I couldn't be happier to have that role.

To my beautiful daughter: Before you were born, I had no idea being a mom could be so wonderful. Thank you for being the best daughter a mom could ever ask for.

And lastly, to my husband, Tom Adams: This book would not have been possible without all your love and encouragement. Thank you from the bottom of my heart. I'm the luckiest woman in the world to have you as my partner in life and work.

* * * * * * * *

59916101R00132

Made in the USA
Charleston, SC
17 August 2016